MENTORING JOURNAL

for

_____

From _____ To _____

TSG TOOLS

For

Teaching Self-Government

ISBN-13: 978-1492180043

ISBN-10: 1492180041

MENTORING FOR
SELF-GOVERNING CHILDREN
AND HAPPY HOMES

Mentor Sessions

Mentor Sessions are only part of the Teaching Self-Government system for raising responsible, happy children. To learn about the rest of this effective approach to parenting visit www.teachingselfgovernment.com and sign up for the newsletter and the Implementation Course. These two things will help put your family in order for greater unity, happiness and true achievement.

Overview of Mentor Sessions

Mentor sessions are designed to help children live productive lives. These meetings give them an opportunity to see a problem in their own life and fix it. Mentor sessions give children connection to parents and focus for life. Here is a brief overview of these sessions:
- Start with the youngest child and work up to the oldest.
- The tone of mentor sessions should be positive and light. This help to motivate the child.
- A record is made for each session (using this book or your own form).
- Sessions last 15-30 minutes.
- One or both parents are present.
- Topics covered usually are: exciting news (things important to the child), projects the child is working on, friends, behavioral goals, academic goals, religious goals, and family goals.
- If applicable a Daddy (or Mommy) Date is planned.

To read more details about mentor sessions, purchase a copy of "Parenting: A House United," by Nicholeen Peck

Mentor Sessions Outline and Tips

Leader of Mentor Sessions
- Which parent needs more one-on-one time with the child? That's the parent who should lead the Mentor Session.
- The other parent stays quiet and listens, unless asked for input.

Length of the Mentor Session
- The length of the Mentor Sessions varies depending upon the age and needs of each child. A good rule of thumb is 15-30 minutes for each session.
- NOTE: We usually we take a lot more time — sometimes even double the time — for Mentor Sessions. We've found that our children love having solo time with Dad and Mom so much that they don't want it to end.

Topics to Discuss
1. **Exciting News:**
   - "What is your exciting news this week?"
   - NOTE: If your child doesn't think anything in life is worth appreciating or getting excited about, your child may be too spoiled. Ingratitude is a sign of a weak character. The antidote for a sick character is good hard work. If your child thinks life is boring, or that nothing exciting happens, then you need to make sure he or she understands what real work feels like so that the child learns to appreciate regular life and the small,

everyday miracles and blessings of life. Teach your children to work by having family work times. Work with your children. Tackle large projects, get dirty together and avoid power struggles. Hard work situations bond family members.

2. **Goals:** Goals are lists of things we hope to accomplish. We try for goals, but don't have any synthetic consequences attached to not accomplishing goals.
   - Ask how your children are progressing on their religious goals (memorizing, certifications, religious awards, Boy or Cub Scouts, etc.) .
   - After checking each child's progress on religious goals (which could be as easy as hearing a memorized church song or scripture — or as complex as checking through a list of accomplishments), take some time to set new church goals for the new week.

3. **Behaviors/Friends/Family/Concerns/Decisions:** This section is designed to open the conversation up for discussing problem behaviors, peer issues or concerns, family troubles or concerns, any other general concerns, and what decisions have been made to practice better self-government skills concerning these areas of concern or problems.
   - If a child has a problem with lying, not being respectful, or getting along well with friends or siblings, this is a good time to set a self-government goal for the week.
   - Some behaviors will take more reminders than once a week, but this time can be the big goal-making time; the other times can just be check-ups.
   - During this meeting the parent can say, "I've noticed you have had a hard time getting along with your friend Billy lately. Is everything okay?" If the child says his relationship with Billy isn't doing very well, then the parent can say, "A good way to show Billy that you like him and want to be his friend is to give Billy compliments instead of saying mean things." Another child might need to hear, "These past few days you have had a hard time staying on task when you're given an instruction. What kind of a positive consequence could we decide upon to help you want to choose to stay on task?" These are the kinds of short, sweet, pointed questions that encourage children to take a leading role in mastering their own behaviors and relationships.

4. **Education**
   - A big part of the form is dedicated to education. Parents can make a big difference in the education of their children. Teachers will tell you that parents who are involved in their child's educational process usually have smarter, more well mannered and accomplished children.
   - First review the previous week's educational goals by saying, "Last week you made a goal to…how have you done on that goal?" Asking for a report of the previous week reminds the child that the next week you will want to know how well he/she did on his/her new goals. Reporting gives the child a reason to stay focused on the goal
   - Five great questions to ask:
     1. What have you been working on lately at school?
     2. What is exciting to you?
     3. What do you want to know more about or improve at?
     4. What do you want to have more time to do?
     5. What subject do you know needs the most of your attention right now?
   - This reporting time also offers a great time to problem solve real-life situations. Was the goal reasonable to accomplish in one week? Did I pick the right time to accomplish the goal? Do I need any other skills or help to complete this goal? Should I try to accomplish this goal a little bit at a time?

5. **Commitments**
   - As children mature, they will show that they are ready to start making commitments, which are more than goals. The youth show us they are ready to start making commitments by being really focused on the goals they set, and by wanting to study more hours in the day. The youth start having plans about their future, so studying and goal setting are suddenly really important. This kind of a youth will do well with commitments because they will want to accomplish them. Commitments can also work for youth who are having a hard time being motivated. But if commitments aren't really taken seriously by the youth, then you know your

child isn't mature enough to have taken ownership of his own personal development and education yet. At this point you might want to ask yourself and your youth, "What is distracting him/you from keeping his/your educational commitments?" If too much media or social time is to blame, you may want to remove some of the distractions from his life.

- At the commitments section of the form, the youth writes a commitment to do something by a certain time and then signs the form before a witness. Commitments usually also have positive and negative consequences attached to them. So, a commitment might read, "I, Quinton Peck, commit to have five math lessons done by next Friday evening or I will not be able to go to the youth swimming party that's going to be at the city pool. If I do get my math lessons done, I can go to the party and Mom will give me a ride."

6. **Recreation and Play:** Life should be fun and exciting.
   - "It's a good idea to pick something enjoyable that you want to do each week as something to look forward to. What is something fun you would like to do this week?" Help he child set the goal. That way, he helps make sure the goal can become a possibility. Teach the child by example how to make goals realities, while making lasting memories with Dad at the same time.

7. **Daddy/Mommy Dates**
   - Each child gets the opportunity to go on a special date with a parent every four weeks (or whatever works for your family). The dates don't necessarily have to cost anything, or they can be budget for and cost a bit. Here are a few ideas: fishing, shopping, going to the park, attending a class, seeing a theater show, playing a game, or making up a puppet show (and then sharing it with the family).
   - If, for example, you decide to do Daddy/Mommy dates every Thursday, you can decide on Sunday evening the plan for the date — and then your child will greatly anticipate every Thursday evening.

Sessions to Fit Each Child

The mentor sessions are personalized.
- A four-year-old child may start his mentor session by drawing a picture on a blank piece of paper. Then the leader parent and the child discuss the picture and move on to other things, like reading a story together or singing a few songs. A session with a child this young may last 15 minutes.
- A six-year-old's session may also last about 15 minutes
- Older children (10 or older) usually have enough to talk about that 30 minutes seems to work well. During this time they may write down a plan for accomplishing their goals.

Scheduling Mentor Sessions?

- Do what works best for your family. Keep in mind that you should plan to hold Mentor Sessions weekly.
- Many families decide Sunday afternoons are an ideal time to hold a weekly Mentor Session.
- Larger families have often assigned a night of the week to a certain child. On the child's night, the child is allowed to stay up 30 minutes longer before going to bed so that the child can talk with Mom and Dad.

Mentor Session Tips

1. Say less. If the parent says too much, the child turns off and has a bad mentor experience. If you say less, the spirit of your words can be felt as well. Practice saying things in a short, powerful and inspiring way. Get to your point in one to two sentences.
2. Let your child be the talker. To help your child do the talking, ask lots of questions.
3. No lectures. When the child says, "I just didn't get time to finish my religious goal this week," don't lecture about not wasting time. Instead, simply say, "What did you do with your time this week?" Then follow it up with, "What kind of changes are you going to make this next week to accomplish your goals?"
4. If you know sensitive topics may surface, make sure you're meeting in a private place away from other children so no one else hears the conversation.

MENTOR MEETING
Parent and Child Relationship

Date:_____ Parent Conducting:_____

Exciting News:_____
Calendar

Monday	Tuesday	Wednesday	Thursday	Friday	Saturday	Sunday

Progress on Spiritual Goals:_____

New Spiritual Goal:_____

Progress on previous Educational Goals/commitments:_____

New Educational Goals:_____

_____

Personal Growth (Behaviors / Concerns / Decisions / Skills):_____

_____

Social Goals (Family / Friends / Boundaries)_____

_____

This week's Educational Goals:_____

_____

New commitments: I,_____ commit to _____

Signed:_____ Witnessed:_____

Fun Goal for the week:_____

Date with Dad/Mom, if it applies:_____

What do I need from Mom/Dad?_____

How is my relationship to parents and siblings?_____

_____

_____

MENTOR MEETING

Parent and Child Relationship

Date: _____   Parent Conducting: _____

Exciting News: _____

Calendar

Monday	Tuesday	Wednesday	Thursday	Friday	Saturday	Sunday

Progress on Spiritual Goals: _____

New Spiritual Goal: _____

Progress on previous Educational Goals/commitments: _____

New Educational Goals: _____
_____

Personal Growth (Behaviors / Concerns / Decisions / Skills): _____
_____

Social Goals (Family / Friends / Boundaries) _____
_____

This week's Educational Goals: _____
_____

New commitments: I, _____ commit to _____

Signed: _____   Witnessed: _____

Fun Goal for the week: _____

Date with Dad/Mom, if it applies: _____

What do I need from Mom/Dad? _____

How is my relationship to parents and siblings? _____
_____
_____

MENTOR MEETING
Parent and Child Relationship

Date:_____ Parent Conducting:_____

Exciting News:_____
Calendar

Monday	Tuesday	Wednesday	Thursday	Friday	Saturday	Sunday

Progress on Spiritual Goals:_____

New Spiritual Goal:_____

Progress on previous Educational Goals/commitments:_____

New Educational Goals:_____

_____

Personal Growth (Behaviors / Concerns / Decisions / Skills):_____

_____

Social Goals (Family / Friends / Boundaries)_____

_____

This week's Educational Goals:_____

_____

New commitments: I,_____ commit to _____

Signed:_____ Witnessed:_____

Fun Goal for the week:_____

Date with Dad/Mom, if it applies:_____

What do I need from Mom/Dad?_____

How is my relationship to parents and siblings?_____

_____

_____

MENTOR MEETING

Parent and Child Relationship

Date: _____ Parent Conducting: _____

Exciting News: _____

Calendar

Monday	Tuesday	Wednesday	Thursday	Friday	Saturday	Sunday

Progress on Spiritual Goals:_____

New Spiritual Goal: _____

Progress on previous Educational Goals/commitments: _____

New Educational Goals: _____

_____

Personal Growth (Behaviors / Concerns / Decisions / Skills):_____

_____

Social Goals (Family / Friends / Boundaries)_____

_____

This week's Educational Goals:_____

_____

New commitments: I,_____ commit to _____

Signed: _____ Witnessed: _____

Fun Goal for the week: _____

Date with Dad/Mom, if it applies:_____

What do I need from Mom/Dad? _____

How is my relationship to parents and siblings?_____

_____

_____

MENTOR MEETING
Parent and Child Relationship

Date: _____ Parent Conducting: _____

Exciting News: _____

Calendar

Monday	Tuesday	Wednesday	Thursday	Friday	Saturday	Sunday

Progress on Spiritual Goals:_____

New Spiritual Goal: _____

Progress on previous Educational Goals/commitments: _____

New Educational Goals:_____

_____

Personal Growth (Behaviors / Concerns / Decisions / Skills):_____

_____

Social Goals (Family / Friends / Boundaries)_____

_____

This week's Educational Goals:_____

_____

New commitments: I,_____ commit to _____

Signed:_____ Witnessed: _____

Fun Goal for the week:_____

Date with Dad/Mom, if it applies: _____

What do I need from Mom/Dad?_____

How is my relationship to parents and siblings?_____

_____

_____

MENTOR MEETING
Parent and Child Relationship

Date: _____   Parent Conducting: _____

Exciting News: _____

Calendar

Monday	Tuesday	Wednesday	Thursday	Friday	Saturday	Sunday

Progress on Spiritual Goals:_____

New Spiritual Goal:_____

Progress on previous Educational Goals/commitments: _____

New Educational Goals:_____

_____

Personal Growth (Behaviors / Concerns / Decisions / Skills):_____

_____

Social Goals (Family / Friends / Boundaries)_____

_____

This week's Educational Goals:_____

_____

New commitments: I,_____ commit to _____

Signed: _____   Witnessed: _____

Fun Goal for the week: _____

Date with Dad/Mom, if it applies:_____

What do I need from Mom/Dad? _____

How is my relationship to parents and siblings?_____

_____

_____

MENTOR MEETING
Parent and Child Relationship

Date:_____ Parent Conducting:_____

Exciting News:_____
Calendar

Monday	Tuesday	Wednesday	Thursday	Friday	Saturday	Sunday

Progress on Spiritual Goals:_____

New Spiritual Goal: _____

Progress on previous Educational Goals/commitments:_____

New Educational Goals:_____

_____

Personal Growth (Behaviors / Concerns / Decisions / Skills):_____

_____

Social Goals (Family / Friends / Boundaries)_____

_____

This week's Educational Goals:_____

_____

New commitments: I,_____ commit to _____

Signed:_____ Witnessed: _____

Fun Goal for the week: _____

Date with Dad/Mom, if it applies: _____

What do I need from Mom/Dad? _____

How is my relationship to parents and siblings?_____

_____

_____

MENTOR MEETING
Parent and Child Relationship

Date: _____   Parent Conducting: _____

Exciting News: _____
Calendar

Monday	Tuesday	Wednesday	Thursday	Friday	Saturday	Sunday

Progress on Spiritual Goals: _____

New Spiritual Goal: _____

Progress on previous Educational Goals/commitments: _____

New Educational Goals: _____

_____

Personal Growth (Behaviors / Concerns / Decisions / Skills): _____

_____

Social Goals (Family / Friends / Boundaries) _____

_____

This week's Educational Goals: _____

_____

New commitments: I, _____ commit to _____

Signed: _____   Witnessed: _____

Fun Goal for the week: _____

Date with Dad/Mom, if it applies: _____

What do I need from Mom/Dad? _____

How is my relationship to parents and siblings? _____

_____

_____

MENTOR MEETING
Parent and Child Relationship

Date:_____ Parent Conducting: _____

Exciting News: _____

Calendar

Monday	Tuesday	Wednesday	Thursday	Friday	Saturday	Sunday

Progress on Spiritual Goals:_____

New Spiritual Goal: _____

Progress on previous Educational Goals/commitments: _____

New Educational Goals:_____

_____

Personal Growth (Behaviors / Concerns / Decisions / Skills):_____

_____

Social Goals (Family / Friends / Boundaries)_____

_____

This week's Educational Goals:_____

_____

New commitments: I,_____ commit to _____

Signed:_____ Witnessed: _____

Fun Goal for the week:_____

Date with Dad/Mom, if it applies: _____

What do I need from Mom/Dad? _____

How is my relationship to parents and siblings?_____

_____

_____

MENTOR MEETING
Parent and Child Relationship

Date: _____ Parent Conducting: _____

Exciting News: _____

Calendar

Monday	Tuesday	Wednesday	Thursday	Friday	Saturday	Sunday

Progress on Spiritual Goals:_____

New Spiritual Goal: _____

Progress on previous Educational Goals/commitments: _____

New Educational Goals: _____

_____

Personal Growth (Behaviors / Concerns / Decisions / Skills):_____

_____

Social Goals (Family / Friends / Boundaries)_____

_____

This week's Educational Goals: _____

_____

New commitments: I,_____ commit to _____

Signed: _____ Witnessed: _____

Fun Goal for the week: _____

Date with Dad/Mom, if it applies: _____

What do I need from Mom/Dad? _____

How is my relationship to parents and siblings? _____

_____

_____

MENTOR MEETING
Parent and Child Relationship

Date:_____ Parent Conducting:_____

Exciting News:_____

Calendar

Monday	Tuesday	Wednesday	Thursday	Friday	Saturday	Sunday

Progress on Spiritual Goals:_____

New Spiritual Goal:_____

Progress on previous Educational Goals/commitments:_____

New Educational Goals:_____

Personal Growth (Behaviors / Concerns / Decisions / Skills):_____

Social Goals (Family / Friends / Boundaries)_____

This week's Educational Goals:_____

New commitments: I,_____ commit to _____

Signed:_____ Witnessed:_____

Fun Goal for the week:_____

Date with Dad/Mom, if it applies:_____

What do I need from Mom/Dad?_____

How is my relationship to parents and siblings?_____

MENTOR MEETING

Parent and Child Relationship

Date: _____   Parent Conducting: _____

Exciting News: _____

Calendar

Monday	Tuesday	Wednesday	Thursday	Friday	Saturday	Sunday

Progress on Spiritual Goals: _____

New Spiritual Goal: _____

Progress on previous Educational Goals/commitments: _____

New Educational Goals: _____

_____

Personal Growth (Behaviors / Concerns / Decisions / Skills): _____

_____

Social Goals (Family / Friends / Boundaries) _____

_____

This week's Educational Goals: _____

_____

New commitments: I, _____ commit to _____

Signed: _____   Witnessed: _____

Fun Goal for the week: _____

Date with Dad/Mom, if it applies: _____

What do I need from Mom/Dad? _____

How is my relationship to parents and siblings? _____

_____

_____

MENTOR MEETING
Parent and Child Relationship

Date:_____   Parent Conducting: _____

Exciting News: _____
Calendar

Monday	Tuesday	Wednesday	Thursday	Friday	Saturday	Sunday

Progress on Spiritual Goals:_____

New Spiritual Goal: _____

Progress on previous Educational Goals/commitments: _____

New Educational Goals: _____

_____

Personal Growth (Behaviors / Concerns / Decisions / Skills):_____

_____

Social Goals (Family / Friends / Boundaries)_____

_____

This week's Educational Goals:_____

_____

New commitments: I,_____ commit to _____

Signed:_____ Witnessed: _____

Fun Goal for the week: _____

Date with Dad/Mom, if it applies: _____

What do I need from Mom/Dad? _____

How is my relationship to parents and siblings?_____

_____

_____

MENTOR MEETING
Parent and Child Relationship

Date: _____   Parent Conducting: _____

Exciting News: _____

Calendar

Monday	Tuesday	Wednesday	Thursday	Friday	Saturday	Sunday

Progress on Spiritual Goals: _____

New Spiritual Goal: _____

Progress on previous Educational Goals/commitments: _____

New Educational Goals: _____

_____

Personal Growth (Behaviors / Concerns / Decisions / Skills): _____

_____

Social Goals (Family / Friends / Boundaries) _____

_____

This week's Educational Goals: _____

_____

New commitments: I, _____ commit to _____

Signed: _____   Witnessed: _____

Fun Goal for the week: _____

Date with Dad/Mom, if it applies: _____

What do I need from Mom/Dad? _____

How is my relationship to parents and siblings? _____

_____

_____

MENTOR MEETING
Parent and Child Relationship

Date:_____ Parent Conducting:_____

Exciting News:_____

Calendar

Monday	Tuesday	Wednesday	Thursday	Friday	Saturday	Sunday

Progress on Spiritual Goals:_____

New Spiritual Goal:_____

Progress on previous Educational Goals/commitments:_____

New Educational Goals:_____

_____

Personal Growth (Behaviors / Concerns / Decisions / Skills):_____

_____

Social Goals (Family / Friends / Boundaries)_____

_____

This week's Educational Goals:_____

_____

New commitments: I,_____ commit to _____

Signed:_____ Witnessed:_____

Fun Goal for the week:_____

Date with Dad/Mom, if it applies:_____

What do I need from Mom/Dad?_____

How is my relationship to parents and siblings?_____

_____

_____

MENTOR MEETING
Parent and Child Relationship

Date: _____   Parent Conducting: _____

Exciting News: _____

Calendar

Monday	Tuesday	Wednesday	Thursday	Friday	Saturday	Sunday

Progress on Spiritual Goals: _____

New Spiritual Goal: _____

Progress on previous Educational Goals/commitments: _____

New Educational Goals: _____

_____

Personal Growth (Behaviors / Concerns / Decisions / Skills): _____

_____

Social Goals (Family / Friends / Boundaries) _____

_____

This week's Educational Goals: _____

_____

New commitments: I, _____ commit to _____

Signed: _____   Witnessed: _____

Fun Goal for the week: _____

Date with Dad/Mom, if it applies: _____

What do I need from Mom/Dad? _____

How is my relationship to parents and siblings? _____

_____

_____

MENTOR MEETING
Parent and Child Relationship

Date:_____ Parent Conducting:_____

Exciting News:_____

Calendar

Monday	Tuesday	Wednesday	Thursday	Friday	Saturday	Sunday

Progress on Spiritual Goals:_____

New Spiritual Goal:_____

Progress on previous Educational Goals/commitments:_____

New Educational Goals:_____

_____

Personal Growth (Behaviors / Concerns / Decisions / Skills):_____

_____

Social Goals (Family / Friends / Boundaries)_____

_____

This week's Educational Goals:_____

_____

New commitments: I,_____ commit to _____

Signed:_____ Witnessed:_____

Fun Goal for the week:_____

Date with Dad/Mom, if it applies:_____

What do I need from Mom/Dad?_____

How is my relationship to parents and siblings?_____

_____

_____

MENTOR MEETING

Parent and Child Relationship

Date: _____ Parent Conducting: _____

Exciting News: _____

Calendar

Monday	Tuesday	Wednesday	Thursday	Friday	Saturday	Sunday

Progress on Spiritual Goals: _____

New Spiritual Goal: _____

Progress on previous Educational Goals/commitments: _____

New Educational Goals: _____

Personal Growth (Behaviors / Concerns / Decisions / Skills): _____

Social Goals (Family / Friends / Boundaries) _____

This week's Educational Goals: _____

New commitments: I, _____ commit to _____

Signed: _____ Witnessed: _____

Fun Goal for the week: _____

Date with Dad/Mom, if it applies: _____

What do I need from Mom/Dad? _____

How is my relationship to parents and siblings? _____

MENTOR MEETING
Parent and Child Relationship

Date: _____   Parent Conducting: _____

Exciting News: _____

Calendar

Monday	Tuesday	Wednesday	Thursday	Friday	Saturday	Sunday

Progress on Spiritual Goals: _____

New Spiritual Goal: _____

Progress on previous Educational Goals/commitments: _____

New Educational Goals: _____

_____

Personal Growth (Behaviors / Concerns / Decisions / Skills): _____

_____

Social Goals (Family / Friends / Boundaries) _____

_____

This week's Educational Goals: _____

_____

New commitments: I, _____ commit to _____

Signed: _____   Witnessed: _____

Fun Goal for the week: _____

Date with Dad/Mom, if it applies: _____

What do I need from Mom/Dad? _____

How is my relationship to parents and siblings? _____

_____

_____

MENTOR MEETING
Parent and Child Relationship

Date: _____   Parent Conducting: _____

Exciting News: _____
Calendar

Monday	Tuesday	Wednesday	Thursday	Friday	Saturday	Sunday

Progress on Spiritual Goals:_____

New Spiritual Goal: _____

Progress on previous Educational Goals/commitments: _____

New Educational Goals: _____
_____

Personal Growth (Behaviors / Concerns / Decisions / Skills):_____
_____

Social Goals (Family / Friends / Boundaries)_____
_____

This week's Educational Goals: _____
_____

New commitments: I,_____ commit to _____

Signed: _____   Witnessed: _____

Fun Goal for the week: _____

Date with Dad/Mom, if it applies: _____

What do I need from Mom/Dad? _____

How is my relationship to parents and siblings?_____
_____
_____

MENTOR MEETING
Parent and Child Relationship

Date:_____ Parent Conducting:_____

Exciting News:_____

Calendar

Monday	Tuesday	Wednesday	Thursday	Friday	Saturday	Sunday

Progress on Spiritual Goals:_____

New Spiritual Goal:_____

Progress on previous Educational Goals/commitments:_____

New Educational Goals:_____

_____

Personal Growth (Behaviors / Concerns / Decisions / Skills):_____

_____

Social Goals (Family / Friends / Boundaries)_____

_____

This week's Educational Goals:_____

_____

New commitments: I,_____ commit to _____

Signed:_____ Witnessed:_____

Fun Goal for the week:_____

Date with Dad/Mom, if it applies:_____

What do I need from Mom/Dad?_____

How is my relationship to parents and siblings?_____

_____

_____

MENTOR MEETING

Parent and Child Relationship

Date: _____   Parent Conducting: _____

Exciting News: _____

Calendar

Monday	Tuesday	Wednesday	Thursday	Friday	Saturday	Sunday

Progress on Spiritual Goals: _____

New Spiritual Goal: _____

Progress on previous Educational Goals/commitments: _____

New Educational Goals: _____
_____

Personal Growth (Behaviors / Concerns / Decisions / Skills): _____
_____

Social Goals (Family / Friends / Boundaries) _____
_____

This week's Educational Goals: _____
_____

New commitments: I, _____ commit to _____

Signed: _____   Witnessed: _____

Fun Goal for the week: _____

Date with Dad/Mom, if it applies: _____

What do I need from Mom/Dad? _____

How is my relationship to parents and siblings? _____
_____
_____

MENTOR MEETING

Parent and Child Relationship

Date:_____ Parent Conducting:_____

Exciting News:_____

Calendar

Monday	Tuesday	Wednesday	Thursday	Friday	Saturday	Sunday

Progress on Spiritual Goals:_____

New Spiritual Goal:_____

Progress on previous Educational Goals/commitments:_____

New Educational Goals:_____

_____

Personal Growth (Behaviors / Concerns / Decisions / Skills):_____

_____

Social Goals (Family / Friends / Boundaries)_____

_____

This week's Educational Goals:_____

_____

New commitments: I,_____ commit to _____

Signed:_____ Witnessed:_____

Fun Goal for the week:_____

Date with Dad/Mom, if it applies:_____

What do I need from Mom/Dad?_____

How is my relationship to parents and siblings?_____

_____

_____

MENTOR MEETING
Parent and Child Relationship

Date: _____   Parent Conducting: _____

Exciting News: _____

Calendar

Monday	Tuesday	Wednesday	Thursday	Friday	Saturday	Sunday

Progress on Spiritual Goals: _____

New Spiritual Goal: _____

Progress on previous Educational Goals/commitments: _____

New Educational Goals: _____

_____

Personal Growth (Behaviors / Concerns / Decisions / Skills): _____

_____

Social Goals (Family / Friends / Boundaries) _____

_____

This week's Educational Goals: _____

_____

New commitments: I, _____ commit to _____

Signed: _____   Witnessed: _____

Fun Goal for the week: _____

Date with Dad/Mom, if it applies: _____

What do I need from Mom/Dad? _____

How is my relationship to parents and siblings? _____

_____

_____

MENTOR MEETING

Parent and Child Relationship

Date:_____ Parent Conducting:_____

Exciting News:_____

Calendar

Monday	Tuesday	Wednesday	Thursday	Friday	Saturday	Sunday

Progress on Spiritual Goals:_____

New Spiritual Goal:_____

Progress on previous Educational Goals/commitments:_____

New Educational Goals:_____

_____

Personal Growth (Behaviors / Concerns / Decisions / Skills):_____

_____

Social Goals (Family / Friends / Boundaries)_____

_____

This week's Educational Goals:_____

_____

New commitments: I,_____ commit to _____

Signed:_____ Witnessed:_____

Fun Goal for the week:_____

Date with Dad/Mom, if it applies:_____

What do I need from Mom/Dad?_____

How is my relationship to parents and siblings?_____

_____

_____

MENTOR MEETING

Parent and Child Relationship

Date: _____ Parent Conducting: _____

Exciting News: _____

Calendar

Monday	Tuesday	Wednesday	Thursday	Friday	Saturday	Sunday

Progress on Spiritual Goals: _____

New Spiritual Goal: _____

Progress on previous Educational Goals/commitments: _____

New Educational Goals: _____

_____

Personal Growth (Behaviors / Concerns / Decisions / Skills): _____

_____

Social Goals (Family / Friends / Boundaries) _____

_____

This week's Educational Goals: _____

_____

New commitments: I, _____ commit to _____

Signed: _____ Witnessed: _____

Fun Goal for the week: _____

Date with Dad/Mom, if it applies: _____

What do I need from Mom/Dad? _____

How is my relationship to parents and siblings? _____

_____

_____

MENTOR MEETING
Parent and Child Relationship

Date:_____ Parent Conducting: _____

Exciting News: _____

Calendar

Monday	Tuesday	Wednesday	Thursday	Friday	Saturday	Sunday

Progress on Spiritual Goals:_____

New Spiritual Goal: _____

Progress on previous Educational Goals/commitments: _____

New Educational Goals: _____

_____

Personal Growth (Behaviors / Concerns / Decisions / Skills): _____

_____

Social Goals (Family / Friends / Boundaries)_____

_____

This week's Educational Goals: _____

_____

New commitments: I,_____ commit to _____

Signed:_____ Witnessed: _____

Fun Goal for the week: _____

Date with Dad/Mom, if it applies: _____

What do I need from Mom/Dad? _____

How is my relationship to parents and siblings?_____

_____

_____

MENTOR MEETING
Parent and Child Relationship

Date: _____   Parent Conducting: _____

Exciting News: _____

Calendar

Monday	Tuesday	Wednesday	Thursday	Friday	Saturday	Sunday

Progress on Spiritual Goals: _____

New Spiritual Goal: _____

Progress on previous Educational Goals/commitments: _____

New Educational Goals: _____
_____

Personal Growth (Behaviors / Concerns / Decisions / Skills): _____
_____

Social Goals (Family / Friends / Boundaries) _____
_____

This week's Educational Goals: _____
_____

New commitments: I, _____ commit to _____

Signed: _____   Witnessed: _____

Fun Goal for the week: _____

Date with Dad/Mom, if it applies: _____

What do I need from Mom/Dad? _____

How is my relationship to parents and siblings? _____
_____
_____

MENTOR MEETING
Parent and Child Relationship

Date:_____ Parent Conducting:_____

Exciting News:_____
Calendar

Monday	Tuesday	Wednesday	Thursday	Friday	Saturday	Sunday

Progress on Spiritual Goals:_____

New Spiritual Goal:_____

Progress on previous Educational Goals/commitments:_____

New Educational Goals:_____

_____

Personal Growth (Behaviors / Concerns / Decisions / Skills):_____

_____

Social Goals (Family / Friends / Boundaries)_____

_____

This week's Educational Goals:_____

_____

New commitments: I,_____ commit to _____

Signed:_____ Witnessed:_____

Fun Goal for the week:_____

Date with Dad/Mom, if it applies:_____

What do I need from Mom/Dad?_____

How is my relationship to parents and siblings?_____

_____

_____

MENTOR MEETING
Parent and Child Relationship

Date: _____   Parent Conducting: _____

Exciting News: _____

Calendar

Monday	Tuesday	Wednesday	Thursday	Friday	Saturday	Sunday

Progress on Spiritual Goals: _____

New Spiritual Goal: _____

Progress on previous Educational Goals/commitments: _____

New Educational Goals: _____
_____

Personal Growth (Behaviors / Concerns / Decisions / Skills): _____
_____

Social Goals (Family / Friends / Boundaries) _____
_____

This week's Educational Goals: _____
_____

New commitments: I, _____ commit to _____

Signed: _____   Witnessed: _____

Fun Goal for the week: _____

Date with Dad/Mom, if it applies: _____

What do I need from Mom/Dad? _____

How is my relationship to parents and siblings? _____
_____
_____

MENTOR MEETING
Parent and Child Relationship

Date:_____ Parent Conducting:_____

Exciting News:_____

Calendar

Monday	Tuesday	Wednesday	Thursday	Friday	Saturday	Sunday

Progress on Spiritual Goals:_____

New Spiritual Goal:_____

Progress on previous Educational Goals/commitments:_____

New Educational Goals:_____

_____

Personal Growth (Behaviors / Concerns / Decisions / Skills):_____

_____

Social Goals (Family / Friends / Boundaries)_____

_____

This week's Educational Goals:_____

_____

New commitments: I,_____ commit to _____

Signed:_____ Witnessed:_____

Fun Goal for the week:_____

Date with Dad/Mom, if it applies:_____

What do I need from Mom/Dad?_____

How is my relationship to parents and siblings?_____

_____

_____

MENTOR MEETING

Parent and Child Relationship

Date: _____ Parent Conducting: _____

Exciting News: _____

Calendar

Monday	Tuesday	Wednesday	Thursday	Friday	Saturday	Sunday

Progress on Spiritual Goals: _____

New Spiritual Goal: _____

Progress on previous Educational Goals/commitments: _____

New Educational Goals: _____
_____

Personal Growth (Behaviors / Concerns / Decisions / Skills): _____
_____

Social Goals (Family / Friends / Boundaries) _____
_____

This week's Educational Goals: _____
_____

New commitments: I, _____ commit to _____

Signed: _____ Witnessed: _____

Fun Goal for the week: _____

Date with Dad/Mom, if it applies: _____

What do I need from Mom/Dad? _____

How is my relationship to parents and siblings? _____
_____
_____

MENTOR MEETING
Parent and Child Relationship

Date: _____ Parent Conducting: _____

Exciting News: _____

Calendar

Monday	Tuesday	Wednesday	Thursday	Friday	Saturday	Sunday

Progress on Spiritual Goals: _____

New Spiritual Goal: _____

Progress on previous Educational Goals/commitments: _____

New Educational Goals: _____

_____

Personal Growth (Behaviors / Concerns / Decisions / Skills): _____

_____

Social Goals (Family / Friends / Boundaries) _____

_____

This week's Educational Goals: _____

_____

New commitments: I, _____ commit to _____

Signed: _____ Witnessed: _____

Fun Goal for the week: _____

Date with Dad/Mom, if it applies: _____

What do I need from Mom/Dad? _____

How is my relationship to parents and siblings? _____

_____

_____

MENTOR MEETING

Parent and Child Relationship

Date: _____   Parent Conducting: _____

Exciting News: _____

Calendar

Monday	Tuesday	Wednesday	Thursday	Friday	Saturday	Sunday

Progress on Spiritual Goals: _____

New Spiritual Goal: _____

Progress on previous Educational Goals/commitments: _____

New Educational Goals: _____

_____

Personal Growth (Behaviors / Concerns / Decisions / Skills): _____

_____

Social Goals (Family / Friends / Boundaries) _____

_____

This week's Educational Goals: _____

_____

New commitments: I, _____ commit to _____

Signed: _____   Witnessed: _____

Fun Goal for the week: _____

Date with Dad/Mom, if it applies: _____

What do I need from Mom/Dad? _____

How is my relationship to parents and siblings? _____

_____

_____

MENTOR MEETING
Parent and Child Relationship

Date:_____   Parent Conducting:_____

Exciting News:_____

Calendar

Monday	Tuesday	Wednesday	Thursday	Friday	Saturday	Sunday

Progress on Spiritual Goals:_____

New Spiritual Goal:_____

Progress on previous Educational Goals/commitments:_____

New Educational Goals:_____

_____

Personal Growth (Behaviors / Concerns / Decisions / Skills):_____

_____

Social Goals (Family / Friends / Boundaries)_____

_____

This week's Educational Goals:_____

_____

New commitments: I,_____ commit to _____

Signed:_____   Witnessed:_____

Fun Goal for the week:_____

Date with Dad/Mom, if it applies:_____

What do I need from Mom/Dad?_____

How is my relationship to parents and siblings?_____

_____

_____

MENTOR MEETING

Parent and Child Relationship

Date: _____   Parent Conducting: _____

Exciting News: _____

Calendar

Monday	Tuesday	Wednesday	Thursday	Friday	Saturday	Sunday

Progress on Spiritual Goals: _____

New Spiritual Goal: _____

Progress on previous Educational Goals/commitments: _____

New Educational Goals: _____

_____

Personal Growth (Behaviors / Concerns / Decisions / Skills): _____

_____

Social Goals (Family / Friends / Boundaries) _____

_____

This week's Educational Goals: _____

_____

New commitments: I, _____ commit to _____

Signed: _____   Witnessed: _____

Fun Goal for the week: _____

Date with Dad/Mom, if it applies: _____

What do I need from Mom/Dad? _____

How is my relationship to parents and siblings? _____

_____

_____

MENTOR MEETING
Parent and Child Relationship

Date:_____ Parent Conducting:_____

Exciting News:_____
Calendar

Monday	Tuesday	Wednesday	Thursday	Friday	Saturday	Sunday

Progress on Spiritual Goals:_____

New Spiritual Goal:_____

Progress on previous Educational Goals/commitments:_____

New Educational Goals:_____

_____

Personal Growth (Behaviors / Concerns / Decisions / Skills):_____

_____

Social Goals (Family / Friends / Boundaries)_____

_____

This week's Educational Goals:_____

_____

New commitments: I,_____ commit to _____

Signed:_____ Witnessed:_____

Fun Goal for the week:_____

Date with Dad/Mom, if it applies: _____

What do I need from Mom/Dad?_____

How is my relationship to parents and siblings?_____

_____

_____

MENTOR MEETING
Parent and Child Relationship

Date: _____   Parent Conducting: _____

Exciting News: _____
Calendar

Monday	Tuesday	Wednesday	Thursday	Friday	Saturday	Sunday

Progress on Spiritual Goals: _____

New Spiritual Goal: _____

Progress on previous Educational Goals/commitments: _____

New Educational Goals: _____
_____

Personal Growth (Behaviors / Concerns / Decisions / Skills): _____
_____

Social Goals (Family / Friends / Boundaries) _____
_____

This week's Educational Goals: _____
_____

New commitments: I, _____ commit to _____

Signed: _____   Witnessed: _____

Fun Goal for the week: _____

Date with Dad/Mom, if it applies: _____

What do I need from Mom/Dad? _____

How is my relationship to parents and siblings? _____
_____
_____

MENTOR MEETING
Parent and Child Relationship

Date:_____ Parent Conducting:_____

Exciting News:_____

Calendar

Monday	Tuesday	Wednesday	Thursday	Friday	Saturday	Sunday

Progress on Spiritual Goals:_____

New Spiritual Goal:_____

Progress on previous Educational Goals/commitments:_____

New Educational Goals:_____

_____

Personal Growth (Behaviors / Concerns / Decisions / Skills):_____

_____

Social Goals (Family / Friends / Boundaries)_____

_____

This week's Educational Goals:_____

_____

New commitments: I,_____ commit to _____

Signed:_____ Witnessed:_____

Fun Goal for the week:_____

Date with Dad/Mom, if it applies:_____

What do I need from Mom/Dad?_____

How is my relationship to parents and siblings?_____

_____

_____

MENTOR MEETING

Parent and Child Relationship

Date: _____   Parent Conducting: _____

Exciting News: _____

Calendar

Monday	Tuesday	Wednesday	Thursday	Friday	Saturday	Sunday

Progress on Spiritual Goals: _____

New Spiritual Goal: _____

Progress on previous Educational Goals/commitments: _____

New Educational Goals: _____

_____

Personal Growth (Behaviors / Concerns / Decisions / Skills): _____

_____

Social Goals (Family / Friends / Boundaries) _____

_____

This week's Educational Goals: _____

_____

New commitments: I, _____ commit to _____

Signed: _____   Witnessed: _____

Fun Goal for the week: _____

Date with Dad/Mom, if it applies: _____

What do I need from Mom/Dad? _____

How is my relationship to parents and siblings? _____

_____

_____

MENTOR MEETING
Parent and Child Relationship

Date: _____ Parent Conducting: _____

Exciting News: _____

Calendar

Monday	Tuesday	Wednesday	Thursday	Friday	Saturday	Sunday

Progress on Spiritual Goals: _____

New Spiritual Goal: _____

Progress on previous Educational Goals/commitments: _____

New Educational Goals: _____

_____

Personal Growth (Behaviors / Concerns / Decisions / Skills): _____

_____

Social Goals (Family / Friends / Boundaries) _____

_____

This week's Educational Goals: _____

_____

New commitments: I, _____ commit to _____

Signed: _____ Witnessed: _____

Fun Goal for the week: _____

Date with Dad/Mom, if it applies: _____

What do I need from Mom/Dad? _____

How is my relationship to parents and siblings? _____

_____

_____

MENTOR MEETING
Parent and Child Relationship

Date: _____   Parent Conducting: _____

Exciting News: _____

Calendar

Monday	Tuesday	Wednesday	Thursday	Friday	Saturday	Sunday

Progress on Spiritual Goals: _____

New Spiritual Goal: _____

Progress on previous Educational Goals/commitments: _____

New Educational Goals: _____

_____

Personal Growth (Behaviors / Concerns / Decisions / Skills): _____

_____

Social Goals (Family / Friends / Boundaries) _____

_____

This week's Educational Goals: _____

_____

New commitments: I, _____ commit to _____

Signed: _____   Witnessed: _____

Fun Goal for the week: _____

Date with Dad/Mom, if it applies: _____

What do I need from Mom/Dad? _____

How is my relationship to parents and siblings? _____

_____

_____

MENTOR MEETING
Parent and Child Relationship

Date: _____ Parent Conducting: _____

Exciting News: _____

Calendar

Monday	Tuesday	Wednesday	Thursday	Friday	Saturday	Sunday

Progress on Spiritual Goals: _____

New Spiritual Goal: _____

Progress on previous Educational Goals/commitments: _____

New Educational Goals: _____

_____

Personal Growth (Behaviors / Concerns / Decisions / Skills): _____

_____

Social Goals (Family / Friends / Boundaries) _____

_____

This week's Educational Goals: _____

_____

New commitments: I, _____ commit to _____

Signed: _____ Witnessed: _____

Fun Goal for the week: _____

Date with Dad/Mom, if it applies: _____

What do I need from Mom/Dad? _____

How is my relationship to parents and siblings? _____

_____

_____

MENTOR MEETING
Parent and Child Relationship

Date: _____   Parent Conducting: _____

Exciting News: _____
Calendar

Monday	Tuesday	Wednesday	Thursday	Friday	Saturday	Sunday

Progress on Spiritual Goals: _____

New Spiritual Goal: _____

Progress on previous Educational Goals/commitments: _____

New Educational Goals: _____
_____

Personal Growth (Behaviors / Concerns / Decisions / Skills): _____
_____

Social Goals (Family / Friends / Boundaries) _____
_____

This week's Educational Goals: _____
_____

New commitments: I, _____ commit to _____

Signed: _____   Witnessed: _____

Fun Goal for the week: _____

Date with Dad/Mom, if it applies: _____

What do I need from Mom/Dad? _____

How is my relationship to parents and siblings? _____
_____
_____

MENTOR MEETING
Parent and Child Relationship

Date: _____ Parent Conducting: _____

Exciting News: _____

Calendar

Monday	Tuesday	Wednesday	Thursday	Friday	Saturday	Sunday

Progress on Spiritual Goals: _____

New Spiritual Goal: _____

Progress on previous Educational Goals/commitments: _____

New Educational Goals: _____

_____

Personal Growth (Behaviors / Concerns / Decisions / Skills): _____

_____

Social Goals (Family / Friends / Boundaries) _____

_____

This week's Educational Goals: _____

_____

New commitments: I, _____ commit to _____

Signed: _____ Witnessed: _____

Fun Goal for the week: _____

Date with Dad/Mom, if it applies: _____

What do I need from Mom/Dad? _____

How is my relationship to parents and siblings? _____

_____

_____

MENTOR MEETING
Parent and Child Relationship

Date: _____   Parent Conducting: _____

Exciting News: _____

Calendar

Monday	Tuesday	Wednesday	Thursday	Friday	Saturday	Sunday

Progress on Spiritual Goals: _____

New Spiritual Goal: _____

Progress on previous Educational Goals/commitments: _____

New Educational Goals: _____

_____

Personal Growth (Behaviors / Concerns / Decisions / Skills): _____

_____

Social Goals (Family / Friends / Boundaries) _____

_____

This week's Educational Goals: _____

_____

New commitments: I, _____ commit to _____

Signed: _____ Witnessed: _____

Fun Goal for the week: _____

Date with Dad/Mom, if it applies: _____

What do I need from Mom/Dad? _____

How is my relationship to parents and siblings? _____

_____

_____

MENTOR MEETING
Parent and Child Relationship

Date:_____ Parent Conducting:_____

Exciting News:_____
Calendar

Monday	Tuesday	Wednesday	Thursday	Friday	Saturday	Sunday

Progress on Spiritual Goals:_____

New Spiritual Goal:_____

Progress on previous Educational Goals/commitments:_____

New Educational Goals:_____

_____

Personal Growth (Behaviors / Concerns / Decisions / Skills):_____

_____

Social Goals (Family / Friends / Boundaries)_____

_____

This week's Educational Goals:_____

_____

New commitments: I,_____ commit to _____

Signed:_____ Witnessed:_____

Fun Goal for the week:_____

Date with Dad/Mom, if it applies:_____

What do I need from Mom/Dad?_____

How is my relationship to parents and siblings?_____

_____

_____

MENTOR MEETING

Parent and Child Relationship

Date: _____ Parent Conducting: _____

Exciting News: _____

Calendar

Monday	Tuesday	Wednesday	Thursday	Friday	Saturday	Sunday

Progress on Spiritual Goals: _____

New Spiritual Goal: _____

Progress on previous Educational Goals/commitments: _____

New Educational Goals: _____
_____

Personal Growth (Behaviors / Concerns / Decisions / Skills): _____
_____

Social Goals (Family / Friends / Boundaries) _____
_____

This week's Educational Goals: _____
_____

New commitments: I, _____ commit to _____

Signed: _____ Witnessed: _____

Fun Goal for the week: _____

Date with Dad/Mom, if it applies: _____

What do I need from Mom/Dad? _____

How is my relationship to parents and siblings? _____
_____
_____

MENTOR MEETING
Parent and Child Relationship

Date:_____ Parent Conducting:_____

Exciting News:_____
Calendar

Monday	Tuesday	Wednesday	Thursday	Friday	Saturday	Sunday

Progress on Spiritual Goals:_____

New Spiritual Goal: _____

Progress on previous Educational Goals/commitments: _____

New Educational Goals:_____
_____

Personal Growth (Behaviors / Concerns / Decisions / Skills):_____
_____

Social Goals (Family / Friends / Boundaries)_____
_____

This week's Educational Goals:_____
_____

New commitments: I,_____ commit to _____

Signed: _____ Witnessed: _____

Fun Goal for the week:_____

Date with Dad/Mom, if it applies: _____

What do I need from Mom/Dad?_____

How is my relationship to parents and siblings?_____
_____
_____

MENTOR MEETING

Parent and Child Relationship

Date: _____ Parent Conducting: _____

Exciting News: _____

Calendar

Monday	Tuesday	Wednesday	Thursday	Friday	Saturday	Sunday

Progress on Spiritual Goals: _____

New Spiritual Goal: _____

Progress on previous Educational Goals/commitments: _____

New Educational Goals: _____

_____

Personal Growth (Behaviors / Concerns / Decisions / Skills): _____

_____

Social Goals (Family / Friends / Boundaries) _____

_____

This week's Educational Goals: _____

_____

New commitments: I, _____ commit to _____

Signed: _____ Witnessed: _____

Fun Goal for the week: _____

Date with Dad/Mom, if it applies: _____

What do I need from Mom/Dad? _____

How is my relationship to parents and siblings? _____

_____

_____

MENTOR MEETING
Parent and Child Relationship

Date:_____ Parent Conducting:_____

Exciting News:_____

Calendar

Monday	Tuesday	Wednesday	Thursday	Friday	Saturday	Sunday

Progress on Spiritual Goals:_____

New Spiritual Goal: _____

Progress on previous Educational Goals/commitments: _____

New Educational Goals:_____

_____

Personal Growth (Behaviors / Concerns / Decisions / Skills):_____

_____

Social Goals (Family / Friends / Boundaries)_____

_____

This week's Educational Goals:_____

_____

New commitments: I,_____ commit to _____

Signed:_____ Witnessed:_____

Fun Goal for the week:_____

Date with Dad/Mom, if it applies:_____

What do I need from Mom/Dad?_____

How is my relationship to parents and siblings?_____

_____

_____

MENTOR MEETING
Parent and Child Relationship

Date: _____ Parent Conducting: _____

Exciting News: _____

Calendar

Monday	Tuesday	Wednesday	Thursday	Friday	Saturday	Sunday

Progress on Spiritual Goals:_____

New Spiritual Goal: _____

Progress on previous Educational Goals/commitments: _____

New Educational Goals: _____
_____

Personal Growth (Behaviors / Concerns / Decisions / Skills):_____
_____

Social Goals (Family / Friends / Boundaries)_____
_____

This week's Educational Goals:_____
_____

New commitments: I,_____ commit to _____

Signed: _____ Witnessed: _____

Fun Goal for the week: _____

Date with Dad/Mom, if it applies: _____

What do I need from Mom/Dad? _____

How is my relationship to parents and siblings?_____
_____
_____

MENTOR MEETING
Parent and Child Relationship

Date: _____ Parent Conducting: _____

Exciting News: _____

Calendar

Monday	Tuesday	Wednesday	Thursday	Friday	Saturday	Sunday

Progress on Spiritual Goals:_____

New Spiritual Goal: _____

Progress on previous Educational Goals/commitments: _____

New Educational Goals:_____

_____

Personal Growth (Behaviors / Concerns / Decisions / Skills):_____

_____

Social Goals (Family / Friends / Boundaries)_____

_____

This week's Educational Goals:_____

_____

New commitments: I,_____ commit to _____

Signed:_____ Witnessed: _____

Fun Goal for the week:_____

Date with Dad/Mom, if it applies: _____

What do I need from Mom/Dad?_____

How is my relationship to parents and siblings?_____

_____

_____

MENTOR MEETING

Parent and Child Relationship

Date: _____   Parent Conducting: _____

Exciting News: _____

Calendar

Monday	Tuesday	Wednesday	Thursday	Friday	Saturday	Sunday

Progress on Spiritual Goals: _____

New Spiritual Goal: _____

Progress on previous Educational Goals/commitments: _____

New Educational Goals: _____

_____

Personal Growth (Behaviors / Concerns / Decisions / Skills): _____

_____

Social Goals (Family / Friends / Boundaries) _____

_____

This week's Educational Goals: _____

_____

New commitments: I, _____ commit to _____

Signed: _____   Witnessed: _____

Fun Goal for the week: _____

Date with Dad/Mom, if it applies: _____

What do I need from Mom/Dad? _____

How is my relationship to parents and siblings? _____

_____

_____

MENTOR MEETING
Parent and Child Relationship

Date:_____ Parent Conducting: _____

Exciting News: _____
Calendar

Monday	Tuesday	Wednesday	Thursday	Friday	Saturday	Sunday

Progress on Spiritual Goals:_____

New Spiritual Goal: _____

Progress on previous Educational Goals/commitments: _____

New Educational Goals:_____

_____

Personal Growth (Behaviors / Concerns / Decisions / Skills):_____

_____

Social Goals (Family / Friends / Boundaries)_____

_____

This week's Educational Goals: _____

_____

New commitments: I,_____ commit to _____

Signed: _____ Witnessed: _____

Fun Goal for the week: _____

Date with Dad/Mom, if it applies: _____

What do I need from Mom/Dad? _____

How is my relationship to parents and siblings?_____

_____

_____

MENTOR MEETING
Parent and Child Relationship

Date: _____   Parent Conducting: _____

Exciting News: _____

Calendar

Monday	Tuesday	Wednesday	Thursday	Friday	Saturday	Sunday

Progress on Spiritual Goals: _____

New Spiritual Goal: _____

Progress on previous Educational Goals/commitments: _____

New Educational Goals: _____

_____

Personal Growth (Behaviors / Concerns / Decisions / Skills): _____

_____

Social Goals (Family / Friends / Boundaries) _____

_____

This week's Educational Goals: _____

_____

New commitments: I, _____ commit to _____

Signed: _____   Witnessed: _____

Fun Goal for the week: _____

Date with Dad/Mom, if it applies: _____

What do I need from Mom/Dad? _____

How is my relationship to parents and siblings? _____

_____

_____

MENTOR MEETING
Parent and Child Relationship

Date:_____ Parent Conducting:_____

Exciting News:_____

Calendar

Monday	Tuesday	Wednesday	Thursday	Friday	Saturday	Sunday

Progress on Spiritual Goals:_____

New Spiritual Goal:_____

Progress on previous Educational Goals/commitments:_____

New Educational Goals:_____

_____

Personal Growth (Behaviors / Concerns / Decisions / Skills):_____

_____

Social Goals (Family / Friends / Boundaries)_____

_____

This week's Educational Goals:_____

_____

New commitments: I,_____ commit to _____

Signed:_____ Witnessed:_____

Fun Goal for the week:_____

Date with Dad/Mom, if it applies:_____

What do I need from Mom/Dad?_____

How is my relationship to parents and siblings?_____

_____

_____

MENTOR MEETING
Parent and Child Relationship

Date: _____   Parent Conducting: _____

Exciting News: _____
Calendar

Monday	Tuesday	Wednesday	Thursday	Friday	Saturday	Sunday

Progress on Spiritual Goals: _____

New Spiritual Goal: _____

Progress on previous Educational Goals/commitments: _____

New Educational Goals: _____
_____

Personal Growth (Behaviors / Concerns / Decisions / Skills): _____
_____

Social Goals (Family / Friends / Boundaries) _____
_____

This week's Educational Goals: _____
_____

New commitments: I, _____ commit to _____

Signed: _____   Witnessed: _____

Fun Goal for the week: _____

Date with Dad/Mom, if it applies: _____

What do I need from Mom/Dad? _____

How is my relationship to parents and siblings? _____
_____
_____

MENTOR MEETING
Parent and Child Relationship

Date:_____ Parent Conducting:_____

Exciting News:_____

Calendar

Monday	Tuesday	Wednesday	Thursday	Friday	Saturday	Sunday

Progress on Spiritual Goals:_____

New Spiritual Goal:_____

Progress on previous Educational Goals/commitments:_____

New Educational Goals:_____

_____

Personal Growth (Behaviors / Concerns / Decisions / Skills):_____

_____

Social Goals (Family / Friends / Boundaries)_____

_____

This week's Educational Goals:_____

_____

New commitments: I,_____ commit to _____

Signed:_____ Witnessed:_____

Fun Goal for the week:_____

Date with Dad/Mom, if it applies:_____

What do I need from Mom/Dad?_____

How is my relationship to parents and siblings?_____

_____

_____

MENTOR MEETING
Parent and Child Relationship

Date: _____   Parent Conducting: _____

Exciting News: _____

Calendar

Monday	Tuesday	Wednesday	Thursday	Friday	Saturday	Sunday

Progress on Spiritual Goals:_____

New Spiritual Goal: _____

Progress on previous Educational Goals/commitments: _____

New Educational Goals: _____

_____

Personal Growth (Behaviors / Concerns / Decisions / Skills):_____

_____

Social Goals (Family / Friends / Boundaries)_____

_____

This week's Educational Goals:_____

_____

New commitments: I,_____ commit to _____

Signed: _____   Witnessed: _____

Fun Goal for the week: _____

Date with Dad/Mom, if it applies:_____

What do I need from Mom/Dad? _____

How is my relationship to parents and siblings?_____

_____

_____

MENTOR MEETING
Parent and Child Relationship

Date:_____ Parent Conducting:_____

Exciting News:_____
Calendar

Monday	Tuesday	Wednesday	Thursday	Friday	Saturday	Sunday

Progress on Spiritual Goals:_____

New Spiritual Goal:_____

Progress on previous Educational Goals/commitments:_____

New Educational Goals:_____

Personal Growth (Behaviors / Concerns / Decisions / Skills):_____

Social Goals (Family / Friends / Boundaries)_____

This week's Educational Goals:_____

New commitments: I,_____ commit to _____

Signed:_____ Witnessed:_____

Fun Goal for the week:_____

Date with Dad/Mom, if it applies:_____

What do I need from Mom/Dad?_____

How is my relationship to parents and siblings?_____

MENTOR MEETING
Parent and Child Relationship

Date: _____ Parent Conducting: _____

Exciting News: _____

Calendar

Monday	Tuesday	Wednesday	Thursday	Friday	Saturday	Sunday

Progress on Spiritual Goals: _____

New Spiritual Goal: _____

Progress on previous Educational Goals/commitments: _____

New Educational Goals: _____

_____

Personal Growth (Behaviors / Concerns / Decisions / Skills): _____

_____

Social Goals (Family / Friends / Boundaries) _____

_____

This week's Educational Goals: _____

_____

New commitments: I, _____ commit to _____

Signed: _____ Witnessed: _____

Fun Goal for the week: _____

Date with Dad/Mom, if it applies: _____

What do I need from Mom/Dad? _____

How is my relationship to parents and siblings? _____

_____

_____

MENTOR MEETING
Parent and Child Relationship

Date: _____ Parent Conducting: _____

Exciting News: _____

Calendar

Monday	Tuesday	Wednesday	Thursday	Friday	Saturday	Sunday

Progress on Spiritual Goals: _____

New Spiritual Goal: _____

Progress on previous Educational Goals/commitments: _____

New Educational Goals: _____

_____

Personal Growth (Behaviors / Concerns / Decisions / Skills): _____

_____

Social Goals (Family / Friends / Boundaries) _____

_____

This week's Educational Goals: _____

_____

New commitments: I, _____ commit to _____

Signed: _____ Witnessed: _____

Fun Goal for the week: _____

Date with Dad/Mom, if it applies: _____

What do I need from Mom/Dad? _____

How is my relationship to parents and siblings? _____

_____

_____

MENTOR MEETING
Parent and Child Relationship

Date: _____   Parent Conducting: _____

Exciting News: _____

Calendar

Monday	Tuesday	Wednesday	Thursday	Friday	Saturday	Sunday

Progress on Spiritual Goals: _____

New Spiritual Goal: _____

Progress on previous Educational Goals/commitments: _____

New Educational Goals: _____

_____

Personal Growth (Behaviors / Concerns / Decisions / Skills): _____

_____

Social Goals (Family / Friends / Boundaries) _____

_____

This week's Educational Goals: _____

_____

New commitments: I, _____ commit to _____

Signed: _____   Witnessed: _____

Fun Goal for the week: _____

Date with Dad/Mom, if it applies: _____

What do I need from Mom/Dad? _____

How is my relationship to parents and siblings? _____

_____

_____

MENTOR MEETING
Parent and Child Relationship

Date:_____   Parent Conducting:_____

Exciting News:_____
Calendar

Monday	Tuesday	Wednesday	Thursday	Friday	Saturday	Sunday

Progress on Spiritual Goals:_____

New Spiritual Goal:_____

Progress on previous Educational Goals/commitments:_____

New Educational Goals:_____
_____

Personal Growth (Behaviors / Concerns / Decisions / Skills):_____
_____

Social Goals (Family / Friends / Boundaries)_____
_____

This week's Educational Goals:_____
_____

New commitments: I,_____ commit to _____

Signed:_____   Witnessed:_____

Fun Goal for the week:_____

Date with Dad/Mom, if it applies:_____

What do I need from Mom/Dad?_____

How is my relationship to parents and siblings?_____
_____
_____

MENTOR MEETING
Parent and Child Relationship

Date: _____   Parent Conducting: _____

Exciting News: _____

Calendar

Monday	Tuesday	Wednesday	Thursday	Friday	Saturday	Sunday

Progress on Spiritual Goals: _____

New Spiritual Goal: _____

Progress on previous Educational Goals/commitments: _____

New Educational Goals: _____

_____

Personal Growth (Behaviors / Concerns / Decisions / Skills): _____

_____

Social Goals (Family / Friends / Boundaries) _____

_____

This week's Educational Goals: _____

_____

New commitments: I, _____ commit to _____

Signed: _____   Witnessed: _____

Fun Goal for the week: _____

Date with Dad/Mom, if it applies: _____

What do I need from Mom/Dad? _____

How is my relationship to parents and siblings? _____

_____

_____

MENTOR MEETING

Parent and Child Relationship

Date:_____ Parent Conducting:_____

Exciting News:_____

Calendar

Monday	Tuesday	Wednesday	Thursday	Friday	Saturday	Sunday

Progress on Spiritual Goals:_____

New Spiritual Goal:_____

Progress on previous Educational Goals/commitments:_____

New Educational Goals:_____

_____

Personal Growth (Behaviors / Concerns / Decisions / Skills):_____

_____

Social Goals (Family / Friends / Boundaries)_____

_____

This week's Educational Goals:_____

_____

New commitments: I,_____ commit to _____

Signed:_____ Witnessed:_____

Fun Goal for the week:_____

Date with Dad/Mom, if it applies:_____

What do I need from Mom/Dad?_____

How is my relationship to parents and siblings?_____

_____

_____

MENTOR MEETING
Parent and Child Relationship

Date: _____   Parent Conducting: _____

Exciting News: _____

Calendar

Monday	Tuesday	Wednesday	Thursday	Friday	Saturday	Sunday

Progress on Spiritual Goals:_____

New Spiritual Goal: _____

Progress on previous Educational Goals/commitments: _____

New Educational Goals: _____

_____

Personal Growth (Behaviors / Concerns / Decisions / Skills):_____

_____

Social Goals (Family / Friends / Boundaries)_____

_____

This week's Educational Goals: _____

_____

New commitments: I,_____ commit to _____

Signed: _____ Witnessed: _____

Fun Goal for the week: _____

Date with Dad/Mom, if it applies: _____

What do I need from Mom/Dad? _____

How is my relationship to parents and siblings? _____

_____

_____

MENTOR MEETING

Parent and Child Relationship

Date: _____ Parent Conducting: _____

Exciting News: _____

Calendar

Monday	Tuesday	Wednesday	Thursday	Friday	Saturday	Sunday

Progress on Spiritual Goals: _____

New Spiritual Goal: _____

Progress on previous Educational Goals/commitments: _____

New Educational Goals: _____

_____

Personal Growth (Behaviors / Concerns / Decisions / Skills): _____

_____

Social Goals (Family / Friends / Boundaries) _____

_____

This week's Educational Goals: _____

_____

New commitments: I, _____ commit to _____

Signed: _____ Witnessed: _____

Fun Goal for the week: _____

Date with Dad/Mom, if it applies: _____

What do I need from Mom/Dad? _____

How is my relationship to parents and siblings? _____

_____

_____

MENTOR MEETING
Parent and Child Relationship

Date: _____   Parent Conducting: _____

Exciting News: _____

Calendar

Monday	Tuesday	Wednesday	Thursday	Friday	Saturday	Sunday

Progress on Spiritual Goals: _____

New Spiritual Goal: _____

Progress on previous Educational Goals/commitments: _____

New Educational Goals: _____

_____

Personal Growth (Behaviors / Concerns / Decisions / Skills): _____

_____

Social Goals (Family / Friends / Boundaries) _____

_____

This week's Educational Goals: _____

_____

New commitments: I, _____ commit to _____

Signed: _____   Witnessed: _____

Fun Goal for the week: _____

Date with Dad/Mom, if it applies: _____

What do I need from Mom/Dad? _____

How is my relationship to parents and siblings? _____

_____

_____

MENTOR MEETING
Parent and Child Relationship

Date:_____ Parent Conducting:_____

Exciting News:_____

Calendar

Monday	Tuesday	Wednesday	Thursday	Friday	Saturday	Sunday

Progress on Spiritual Goals:_____

New Spiritual Goal: _____

Progress on previous Educational Goals/commitments:_____

New Educational Goals:_____

_____

Personal Growth (Behaviors / Concerns / Decisions / Skills):_____

_____

Social Goals (Family / Friends / Boundaries)_____

_____

This week's Educational Goals:_____

_____

New commitments: I,_____ commit to _____

Signed:_____ Witnessed:_____

Fun Goal for the week:_____

Date with Dad/Mom, if it applies:_____

What do I need from Mom/Dad?_____

How is my relationship to parents and siblings?_____

_____

_____

MENTOR MEETING
Parent and Child Relationship

Date: _____   Parent Conducting: _____

Exciting News: _____

Calendar

Monday	Tuesday	Wednesday	Thursday	Friday	Saturday	Sunday

Progress on Spiritual Goals: _____

New Spiritual Goal: _____

Progress on previous Educational Goals/commitments: _____

New Educational Goals: _____

_____

Personal Growth (Behaviors / Concerns / Decisions / Skills): _____

_____

Social Goals (Family / Friends / Boundaries) _____

_____

This week's Educational Goals: _____

_____

New commitments: I, _____ commit to _____

Signed: _____   Witnessed: _____

Fun Goal for the week: _____

Date with Dad/Mom, if it applies: _____

What do I need from Mom/Dad? _____

How is my relationship to parents and siblings? _____

_____

_____

MENTOR MEETING
Parent and Child Relationship

Date: _____   Parent Conducting: _____

Exciting News: _____

Calendar

Monday	Tuesday	Wednesday	Thursday	Friday	Saturday	Sunday

Progress on Spiritual Goals: _____

New Spiritual Goal: _____

Progress on previous Educational Goals/commitments: _____

New Educational Goals: _____

_____

Personal Growth (Behaviors / Concerns / Decisions / Skills): _____

_____

Social Goals (Family / Friends / Boundaries) _____

_____

This week's Educational Goals: _____

_____

New commitments: I, _____ commit to _____

Signed: _____   Witnessed: _____

Fun Goal for the week: _____

Date with Dad/Mom, if it applies: _____

What do I need from Mom/Dad? _____

How is my relationship to parents and siblings? _____

_____

_____

MENTOR MEETING
Parent and Child Relationship

Date: _____ Parent Conducting: _____

Exciting News: _____
    Calendar

Monday	Tuesday	Wednesday	Thursday	Friday	Saturday	Sunday

Progress on Spiritual Goals: _____

New Spiritual Goal: _____

Progress on previous Educational Goals/commitments: _____

New Educational Goals: _____
_____

Personal Growth (Behaviors / Concerns / Decisions / Skills): _____
_____

Social Goals (Family / Friends / Boundaries) _____
_____

This week's Educational Goals: _____
_____

New commitments: I, _____ commit to _____

Signed: _____ Witnessed: _____

Fun Goal for the week: _____

Date with Dad/Mom, if it applies: _____

What do I need from Mom/Dad? _____

How is my relationship to parents and siblings? _____
_____
_____

MENTOR MEETING
Parent and Child Relationship

Date:_____ Parent Conducting:_____

Exciting News:_____
Calendar

Monday	Tuesday	Wednesday	Thursday	Friday	Saturday	Sunday

Progress on Spiritual Goals:_____

New Spiritual Goal:_____

Progress on previous Educational Goals/commitments:_____

New Educational Goals:_____

_____

Personal Growth (Behaviors / Concerns / Decisions / Skills):_____

_____

Social Goals (Family / Friends / Boundaries)_____

_____

This week's Educational Goals:_____

_____

New commitments: I,_____ commit to _____

Signed:_____ Witnessed:_____

Fun Goal for the week:_____

Date with Dad/Mom, if it applies:_____

What do I need from Mom/Dad?_____

How is my relationship to parents and siblings?_____

_____

_____

MENTOR MEETING

Parent and Child Relationship

Date: _____ Parent Conducting: _____

Exciting News: _____

Calendar

Monday	Tuesday	Wednesday	Thursday	Friday	Saturday	Sunday

Progress on Spiritual Goals:_____

New Spiritual Goal: _____

Progress on previous Educational Goals/commitments:_____

New Educational Goals:_____

_____

Personal Growth (Behaviors / Concerns / Decisions / Skills):_____

_____

Social Goals (Family / Friends / Boundaries)_____

_____

This week's Educational Goals:_____

_____

New commitments: I,_____ commit to _____

Signed: _____ Witnessed: _____

Fun Goal for the week: _____

Date with Dad/Mom, if it applies:_____

What do I need from Mom/Dad?_____

How is my relationship to parents and siblings?_____

_____

_____

MENTOR MEETING
Parent and Child Relationship

Date:_____ Parent Conducting:_____

Exciting News:_____

Calendar

Monday	Tuesday	Wednesday	Thursday	Friday	Saturday	Sunday

Progress on Spiritual Goals:_____

New Spiritual Goal:_____

Progress on previous Educational Goals/commitments:_____

New Educational Goals:_____

_____

Personal Growth (Behaviors / Concerns / Decisions / Skills):_____

_____

Social Goals (Family / Friends / Boundaries)_____

_____

This week's Educational Goals:_____

_____

New commitments: I,_____ commit to _____

Signed:_____ Witnessed:_____

Fun Goal for the week:_____

Date with Dad/Mom, if it applies:_____

What do I need from Mom/Dad?_____

How is my relationship to parents and siblings?_____

_____

_____

MENTOR MEETING

Parent and Child Relationship

Date: _____   Parent Conducting: _____

Exciting News: _____

Calendar

Monday	Tuesday	Wednesday	Thursday	Friday	Saturday	Sunday

Progress on Spiritual Goals: _____

New Spiritual Goal: _____

Progress on previous Educational Goals/commitments: _____

New Educational Goals: _____

_____

Personal Growth (Behaviors / Concerns / Decisions / Skills): _____

_____

Social Goals (Family / Friends / Boundaries) _____

_____

This week's Educational Goals: _____

_____

New commitments: I, _____ commit to _____

Signed: _____   Witnessed: _____

Fun Goal for the week: _____

Date with Dad/Mom, if it applies: _____

What do I need from Mom/Dad? _____

How is my relationship to parents and siblings? _____

_____

_____

MENTOR MEETING
Parent and Child Relationship

Date: _____ Parent Conducting: _____

Exciting News: _____
Calendar

Monday	Tuesday	Wednesday	Thursday	Friday	Saturday	Sunday

Progress on Spiritual Goals: _____

New Spiritual Goal: _____

Progress on previous Educational Goals/commitments: _____

New Educational Goals: _____

_____

Personal Growth (Behaviors / Concerns / Decisions / Skills): _____

_____

Social Goals (Family / Friends / Boundaries) _____

_____

This week's Educational Goals: _____

_____

New commitments: I, _____ commit to _____

Signed: _____ Witnessed: _____

Fun Goal for the week: _____

Date with Dad/Mom, if it applies: _____

What do I need from Mom/Dad? _____

How is my relationship to parents and siblings? _____

_____

_____

MENTOR MEETING
Parent and Child Relationship

Date: _____   Parent Conducting: _____

Exciting News: _____
Calendar

Monday	Tuesday	Wednesday	Thursday	Friday	Saturday	Sunday

Progress on Spiritual Goals: _____

New Spiritual Goal: _____

Progress on previous Educational Goals/commitments: _____

New Educational Goals: _____
_____

Personal Growth (Behaviors / Concerns / Decisions / Skills): _____
_____

Social Goals (Family / Friends / Boundaries) _____
_____

This week's Educational Goals: _____
_____

New commitments: I, _____ commit to _____

Signed: _____   Witnessed: _____

Fun Goal for the week: _____

Date with Dad/Mom, if it applies: _____

What do I need from Mom/Dad? _____

How is my relationship to parents and siblings? _____
_____
_____

MENTOR MEETING
Parent and Child Relationship

Date: _____ Parent Conducting: _____

Exciting News: _____

Calendar

Monday	Tuesday	Wednesday	Thursday	Friday	Saturday	Sunday

Progress on Spiritual Goals: _____

New Spiritual Goal: _____

Progress on previous Educational Goals/commitments: _____

New Educational Goals: _____

_____

Personal Growth (Behaviors / Concerns / Decisions / Skills): _____

_____

Social Goals (Family / Friends / Boundaries) _____

_____

This week's Educational Goals: _____

_____

New commitments: I, _____ commit to _____

Signed: _____ Witnessed: _____

Fun Goal for the week: _____

Date with Dad/Mom, if it applies: _____

What do I need from Mom/Dad? _____

How is my relationship to parents and siblings? _____

_____

_____

MENTOR MEETING
Parent and Child Relationship

Date: _____ Parent Conducting: _____

Exciting News: _____
Calendar

Monday	Tuesday	Wednesday	Thursday	Friday	Saturday	Sunday

Progress on Spiritual Goals: _____

New Spiritual Goal: _____

Progress on previous Educational Goals/commitments: _____

New Educational Goals: _____
_____

Personal Growth (Behaviors / Concerns / Decisions / Skills): _____
_____

Social Goals (Family / Friends / Boundaries) _____
_____

This week's Educational Goals: _____
_____

New commitments: I, _____ commit to _____

Signed: _____ Witnessed: _____

Fun Goal for the week: _____

Date with Dad/Mom, if it applies: _____

What do I need from Mom/Dad? _____

How is my relationship to parents and siblings? _____
_____
_____

MENTOR MEETING
Parent and Child Relationship

Date: _____ Parent Conducting: _____

Exciting News: _____

Calendar

Monday	Tuesday	Wednesday	Thursday	Friday	Saturday	Sunday

Progress on Spiritual Goals: _____

New Spiritual Goal: _____

Progress on previous Educational Goals/commitments: _____

New Educational Goals: _____

_____

Personal Growth (Behaviors / Concerns / Decisions / Skills): _____

_____

Social Goals (Family / Friends / Boundaries) _____

_____

This week's Educational Goals: _____

_____

New commitments: I, _____ commit to _____

Signed: _____ Witnessed: _____

Fun Goal for the week: _____

Date with Dad/Mom, if it applies: _____

What do I need from Mom/Dad? _____

How is my relationship to parents and siblings? _____

_____

_____

MENTOR MEETING
Parent and Child Relationship

Date: _____   Parent Conducting: _____

Exciting News: _____
Calendar

Monday	Tuesday	Wednesday	Thursday	Friday	Saturday	Sunday

Progress on Spiritual Goals:_____

New Spiritual Goal: _____

Progress on previous Educational Goals/commitments: _____

New Educational Goals: _____

_____

Personal Growth (Behaviors / Concerns / Decisions / Skills):_____

_____

Social Goals (Family / Friends / Boundaries)_____

_____

This week's Educational Goals: _____

_____

New commitments: I,_____ commit to _____

Signed: _____   Witnessed: _____

Fun Goal for the week: _____

Date with Dad/Mom, if it applies: _____

What do I need from Mom/Dad? _____

How is my relationship to parents and siblings? _____

_____

_____

MENTOR MEETING
Parent and Child Relationship

Date:_____ Parent Conducting: _____

Exciting News: _____

Calendar

Monday	Tuesday	Wednesday	Thursday	Friday	Saturday	Sunday

Progress on Spiritual Goals:_____

New Spiritual Goal: _____

Progress on previous Educational Goals/commitments: _____

New Educational Goals:_____

_____

Personal Growth (Behaviors / Concerns / Decisions / Skills):_____

_____

Social Goals (Family / Friends / Boundaries)_____

_____

This week's Educational Goals:_____

_____

New commitments: I,_____ commit to _____

Signed:_____ Witnessed:_____

Fun Goal for the week:_____

Date with Dad/Mom, if it applies: _____

What do I need from Mom/Dad?_____

How is my relationship to parents and siblings?_____

_____

_____

MENTOR MEETING
Parent and Child Relationship

Date: _____   Parent Conducting: _____

Exciting News: _____

Calendar

Monday	Tuesday	Wednesday	Thursday	Friday	Saturday	Sunday

Progress on Spiritual Goals: _____

New Spiritual Goal: _____

Progress on previous Educational Goals/commitments: _____

New Educational Goals: _____
_____

Personal Growth (Behaviors / Concerns / Decisions / Skills): _____
_____

Social Goals (Family / Friends / Boundaries) _____
_____

This week's Educational Goals: _____
_____

New commitments: I, _____ commit to _____

Signed: _____   Witnessed: _____

Fun Goal for the week: _____

Date with Dad/Mom, if it applies: _____

What do I need from Mom/Dad? _____

How is my relationship to parents and siblings? _____
_____
_____

MENTOR MEETING
Parent and Child Relationship

Date: _____   Parent Conducting: _____

Exciting News: _____

Calendar

Monday	Tuesday	Wednesday	Thursday	Friday	Saturday	Sunday

Progress on Spiritual Goals: _____

New Spiritual Goal: _____

Progress on previous Educational Goals/commitments: _____

New Educational Goals: _____

_____

Personal Growth (Behaviors / Concerns / Decisions / Skills): _____

_____

Social Goals (Family / Friends / Boundaries) _____

_____

This week's Educational Goals: _____

_____

New commitments: I, _____ commit to _____

Signed: _____   Witnessed: _____

Fun Goal for the week: _____

Date with Dad/Mom, if it applies: _____

What do I need from Mom/Dad? _____

How is my relationship to parents and siblings? _____

_____

_____

MENTOR MEETING
Parent and Child Relationship

Date: _____   Parent Conducting: _____

Exciting News: _____

Calendar

Monday	Tuesday	Wednesday	Thursday	Friday	Saturday	Sunday

Progress on Spiritual Goals: _____

New Spiritual Goal: _____

Progress on previous Educational Goals/commitments: _____

New Educational Goals: _____

_____

Personal Growth (Behaviors / Concerns / Decisions / Skills): _____

_____

Social Goals (Family / Friends / Boundaries) _____

_____

This week's Educational Goals: _____

_____

New commitments: I, _____ commit to _____

Signed: _____   Witnessed: _____

Fun Goal for the week: _____

Date with Dad/Mom, if it applies: _____

What do I need from Mom/Dad? _____

How is my relationship to parents and siblings? _____

_____

_____

MENTOR MEETING

Parent and Child Relationship

Date: _____ Parent Conducting: _____

Exciting News: _____

Calendar

Monday	Tuesday	Wednesday	Thursday	Friday	Saturday	Sunday

Progress on Spiritual Goals: _____

New Spiritual Goal: _____

Progress on previous Educational Goals/commitments: _____

New Educational Goals: _____

_____

Personal Growth (Behaviors / Concerns / Decisions / Skills): _____

_____

Social Goals (Family / Friends / Boundaries) _____

_____

This week's Educational Goals: _____

_____

New commitments: I, _____ commit to _____

Signed: _____ Witnessed: _____

Fun Goal for the week: _____

Date with Dad/Mom, if it applies: _____

What do I need from Mom/Dad? _____

How is my relationship to parents and siblings? _____

_____

_____

MENTOR MEETING
Parent and Child Relationship

Date: _____   Parent Conducting: _____

Exciting News: _____

Calendar

Monday	Tuesday	Wednesday	Thursday	Friday	Saturday	Sunday

Progress on Spiritual Goals: _____

New Spiritual Goal: _____

Progress on previous Educational Goals/commitments: _____

New Educational Goals: _____

_____

Personal Growth (Behaviors / Concerns / Decisions / Skills): _____

_____

Social Goals (Family / Friends / Boundaries) _____

_____

This week's Educational Goals: _____

_____

New commitments: I, _____ commit to _____

Signed: _____   Witnessed: _____

Fun Goal for the week: _____

Date with Dad/Mom, if it applies: _____

What do I need from Mom/Dad? _____

How is my relationship to parents and siblings? _____

_____

_____

MENTOR MEETING
Parent and Child Relationship

Date:_____ Parent Conducting:_____

Exciting News:_____

Calendar

Monday	Tuesday	Wednesday	Thursday	Friday	Saturday	Sunday

Progress on Spiritual Goals:_____

New Spiritual Goal:_____

Progress on previous Educational Goals/commitments:_____

New Educational Goals:_____

_____

Personal Growth (Behaviors / Concerns / Decisions / Skills):_____

_____

Social Goals (Family / Friends / Boundaries)_____

_____

This week's Educational Goals:_____

_____

New commitments: I,_____ commit to _____

Signed:_____ Witnessed:_____

Fun Goal for the week:_____

Date with Dad/Mom, if it applies:_____

What do I need from Mom/Dad?_____

How is my relationship to parents and siblings?_____

_____

_____

_____

MENTOR MEETING

Parent and Child Relationship

Date: _____   Parent Conducting: _____

Exciting News: _____

Calendar

Monday	Tuesday	Wednesday	Thursday	Friday	Saturday	Sunday

Progress on Spiritual Goals: _____

New Spiritual Goal: _____

Progress on previous Educational Goals/commitments: _____

New Educational Goals: _____

_____

Personal Growth (Behaviors / Concerns / Decisions / Skills): _____

_____

Social Goals (Family / Friends / Boundaries) _____

_____

This week's Educational Goals: _____

_____

New commitments: I, _____ commit to _____

Signed: _____   Witnessed: _____

Fun Goal for the week: _____

Date with Dad/Mom, if it applies: _____

What do I need from Mom/Dad? _____

How is my relationship to parents and siblings? _____

_____

_____

MENTOR MEETING
Parent and Child Relationship

Date: _____ Parent Conducting: _____

Exciting News: _____

Calendar

Monday	Tuesday	Wednesday	Thursday	Friday	Saturday	Sunday

Progress on Spiritual Goals: _____

New Spiritual Goal: _____

Progress on previous Educational Goals/commitments: _____

New Educational Goals: _____

_____

Personal Growth (Behaviors / Concerns / Decisions / Skills): _____

_____

Social Goals (Family / Friends / Boundaries)_____

_____

This week's Educational Goals: _____

_____

New commitments: I, _____ commit to _____

Signed: _____ Witnessed: _____

Fun Goal for the week: _____

Date with Dad/Mom, if it applies: _____

What do I need from Mom/Dad? _____

How is my relationship to parents and siblings? _____

_____

_____

MENTOR MEETING
Parent and Child Relationship

Date: _____   Parent Conducting: _____

Exiting News: _____

Calendar

Monday	Tuesday	Wednesday	Thursday	Friday	Saturday	Sunday

Progress on Spiritual Goals: _____

New Spiritual Goal: _____

Progress on previous Educational Goals/commitments: _____

New Educational Goals: _____

_____

Personal Growth (Behaviors / Concerns / Decisions / Skills): _____

_____

Social Goals (Family / Friends / Boundaries) _____

_____

This week's Educational Goals: _____

_____

New commitments: I, _____ commit to _____

Signed: _____   Witnessed: _____

Fun Goal for the week: _____

Date with Dad/Mom, if it applies: _____

What do I need from Mom/Dad? _____

How is my relationship to parents and siblings? _____

_____

_____

MENTOR MEETING
Parent and Child Relationship

Date:_____ Parent Conducting:_____

Exciting News:_____

Calendar

Monday	Tuesday	Wednesday	Thursday	Friday	Saturday	Sunday

Progress on Spiritual Goals:_____

New Spiritual Goal:_____

Progress on previous Educational Goals/commitments:_____

New Educational Goals:_____
_____

Personal Growth (Behaviors / Concerns / Decisions / Skills):_____
_____

Social Goals (Family / Friends / Boundaries)_____
_____

This week's Educational Goals:_____
_____

New commitments: I,_____ commit to _____

Signed:_____ Witnessed:_____

Fun Goal for the week:_____

Date with Dad/Mom, if it applies:_____

What do I need from Mom/Dad?_____

How is my relationship to parents and siblings?_____
_____
_____

MENTOR MEETING

Parent and Child Relationship

Date: _____   Parent Conducting: _____

Exciting News: _____

Calendar

Monday	Tuesday	Wednesday	Thursday	Friday	Saturday	Sunday

Progress on Spiritual Goals: _____

New Spiritual Goal: _____

Progress on previous Educational Goals/commitments: _____

New Educational Goals: _____

_____

Personal Growth (Behaviors / Concerns / Decisions / Skills): _____

_____

Social Goals (Family / Friends / Boundaries) _____

_____

This week's Educational Goals: _____

_____

New commitments: I, _____ commit to _____

Signed: _____   Witnessed: _____

Fun Goal for the week: _____

Date with Dad/Mom, if it applies: _____

What do I need from Mom/Dad? _____

How is my relationship to parents and siblings? _____

_____

_____

MENTOR MEETING

Parent and Child Relationship

Date: _____ Parent Conducting: _____

Exciting News: _____

Calendar

Monday	Tuesday	Wednesday	Thursday	Friday	Saturday	Sunday

Progress on Spiritual Goals: _____

New Spiritual Goal: _____

Progress on previous Educational Goals/commitments: _____

New Educational Goals: _____

_____

Personal Growth (Behaviors / Concerns / Decisions / Skills): _____

_____

Social Goals (Family / Friends / Boundaries) _____

_____

This week's Educational Goals: _____

_____

New commitments: I, _____ commit to _____

Signed: _____ Witnessed: _____

Fun Goal for the week: _____

Date with Dad/Mom, if it applies: _____

What do I need from Mom/Dad? _____

How is my relationship to parents and siblings? _____

_____

_____

MENTOR MEETING
Parent and Child Relationship

Date: _____   Parent Conducting: _____

Exciting News: _____

Calendar

Monday	Tuesday	Wednesday	Thursday	Friday	Saturday	Sunday

Progress on Spiritual Goals: _____

New Spiritual Goal: _____

Progress on previous Educational Goals/commitments: _____

New Educational Goals: _____

_____

Personal Growth (Behaviors / Concerns / Decisions / Skills): _____

_____

Social Goals (Family / Friends / Boundaries) _____

_____

This week's Educational Goals: _____

_____

New commitments: I, _____ commit to _____

Signed: _____   Witnessed: _____

Fun Goal for the week: _____

Date with Dad/Mom, if it applies: _____

What do I need from Mom/Dad? _____

How is my relationship to parents and siblings? _____

_____

_____

MENTOR MEETING
Parent and Child Relationship

Date: _____   Parent Conducting: _____

Exciting News: _____

Calendar

Monday	Tuesday	Wednesday	Thursday	Friday	Saturday	Sunday

Progress on Spiritual Goals: _____

New Spiritual Goal: _____

Progress on previous Educational Goals/commitments: _____

New Educational Goals: _____

_____

Personal Growth (Behaviors / Concerns / Decisions / Skills): _____

_____

Social Goals (Family / Friends / Boundaries) _____

_____

This week's Educational Goals: _____

_____

New commitments: I, _____ commit to _____

Signed: _____   Witnessed: _____

Fun Goal for the week: _____

Date with Dad/Mom, if it applies: _____

What do I need from Mom/Dad? _____

How is my relationship to parents and siblings? _____

_____

_____

MENTOR MEETING
Parent and Child Relationship

Date: _____   Parent Conducting: _____

Exciting News: _____

Calendar

Monday	Tuesday	Wednesday	Thursday	Friday	Saturday	Sunday

Progress on Spiritual Goals: _____

New Spiritual Goal: _____

Progress on previous Educational Goals/commitments: _____

New Educational Goals: _____

_____

Personal Growth (Behaviors / Concerns / Decisions / Skills): _____

_____

Social Goals (Family / Friends / Boundaries) _____

_____

This week's Educational Goals: _____

_____

New commitments: I, _____ commit to _____

Signed: _____   Witnessed: _____

Fun Goal for the week: _____

Date with Dad/Mom, if it applies: _____

What do I need from Mom/Dad? _____

How is my relationship to parents and siblings? _____

_____

_____

MENTOR MEETING
Parent and Child Relationship

Date:_____ Parent Conducting:_____

Exciting News:_____

Calendar

Monday	Tuesday	Wednesday	Thursday	Friday	Saturday	Sunday

Progress on Spiritual Goals:_____

New Spiritual Goal:_____

Progress on previous Educational Goals/commitments:_____

New Educational Goals:_____

_____

Personal Growth (Behaviors / Concerns / Decisions / Skills):_____

_____

Social Goals (Family / Friends / Boundaries)_____

_____

This week's Educational Goals:_____

_____

New commitments: I,_____ commit to _____

Signed:_____ Witnessed:_____

Fun Goal for the week:_____

Date with Dad/Mom, if it applies:_____

What do I need from Mom/Dad?_____

How is my relationship to parents and siblings?_____

_____

_____

MENTOR MEETING

Parent and Child Relationship

Date: _____   Parent Conducting: _____

Exciting News: _____

Calendar

Monday	Tuesday	Wednesday	Thursday	Friday	Saturday	Sunday

Progress on Spiritual Goals: _____

New Spiritual Goal: _____

Progress on previous Educational Goals/commitments: _____

New Educational Goals: _____

_____

Personal Growth (Behaviors / Concerns / Decisions / Skills): _____

_____

Social Goals (Family / Friends / Boundaries) _____

_____

This week's Educational Goals: _____

_____

New commitments: I, _____ commit to _____

Signed: _____   Witnessed: _____

Fun Goal for the week: _____

Date with Dad/Mom, if it applies: _____

What do I need from Mom/Dad? _____

How is my relationship to parents and siblings? _____

_____

_____

MENTOR MEETING
Parent and Child Relationship

Date: _____ Parent Conducting: _____

Exciting News: _____
Calendar

Monday	Tuesday	Wednesday	Thursday	Friday	Saturday	Sunday

Progress on Spiritual Goals: _____

New Spiritual Goal: _____

Progress on previous Educational Goals/commitments: _____

New Educational Goals: _____

_____

Personal Growth (Behaviors / Concerns / Decisions / Skills): _____

_____

Social Goals (Family / Friends / Boundaries) _____

_____

This week's Educational Goals: _____

_____

New commitments: I, _____ commit to _____

Signed: _____ Witnessed: _____

Fun Goal for the week: _____

Date with Dad/Mom, if it applies: _____

What do I need from Mom/Dad? _____

How is my relationship to parents and siblings? _____

_____

_____

MENTOR MEETING

Parent and Child Relationship

Date: _____   Parent Conducting: _____

Exciting News: _____
    Calendar

Monday	Tuesday	Wednesday	Thursday	Friday	Saturday	Sunday

Progress on Spiritual Goals: _____

New Spiritual Goal: _____

Progress on previous Educational Goals/commitments: _____

New Educational Goals: _____
_____

Personal Growth (Behaviors / Concerns / Decisions / Skills): _____
_____

Social Goals (Family / Friends / Boundaries) _____
_____

This week's Educational Goals: _____
_____

New commitments: I, _____ commit to _____

Signed: _____   Witnessed: _____

Fun Goal for the week: _____

Date with Dad/Mom, if it applies: _____

What do I need from Mom/Dad? _____

How is my relationship to parents and siblings? _____
_____
_____

MENTOR MEETING
Parent and Child Relationship

Date:_____ Parent Conducting:_____

Exciting News:_____
Calendar

Monday	Tuesday	Wednesday	Thursday	Friday	Saturday	Sunday

Progress on Spiritual Goals:_____

New Spiritual Goal: _____

Progress on previous Educational Goals/commitments:_____

New Educational Goals:_____

_____

Personal Growth (Behaviors / Concerns / Decisions / Skills):_____

_____

Social Goals (Family / Friends / Boundaries)_____

_____

This week's Educational Goals:_____

_____

New commitments: I,_____ commit to _____

Signed:_____ Witnessed:_____

Fun Goal for the week:_____

Date with Dad/Mom, if it applies: _____

What do I need from Mom/Dad?_____

How is my relationship to parents and siblings?_____

_____

_____

MENTOR MEETING

Parent and Child Relationship

Date: _____ Parent Conducting: _____

Exciting News: _____

Calendar

Monday	Tuesday	Wednesday	Thursday	Friday	Saturday	Sunday

Progress on Spiritual Goals: _____

New Spiritual Goal: _____

Progress on previous Educational Goals/commitments: _____

New Educational Goals: _____

_____

Personal Growth (Behaviors / Concerns / Decisions / Skills): _____

_____

Social Goals (Family / Friends / Boundaries) _____

_____

This week's Educational Goals: _____

_____

New commitments: I, _____ commit to _____

Signed: _____ Witnessed: _____

Fun Goal for the week: _____

Date with Dad/Mom, if it applies: _____

What do I need from Mom/Dad? _____

How is my relationship to parents and siblings? _____

_____

_____

MENTOR MEETING
Parent and Child Relationship

Date:_____ Parent Conducting:_____

Exciting News:_____

Calendar

Monday	Tuesday	Wednesday	Thursday	Friday	Saturday	Sunday

Progress on Spiritual Goals:_____

New Spiritual Goal:_____

Progress on previous Educational Goals/commitments:_____

New Educational Goals:_____

_____

Personal Growth (Behaviors / Concerns / Decisions / Skills):_____

_____

Social Goals (Family / Friends / Boundaries)_____

_____

This week's Educational Goals:_____

_____

New commitments: I,_____ commit to _____

Signed:_____ Witnessed:_____

Fun Goal for the week:_____

Date with Dad/Mom, if it applies:_____

What do I need from Mom/Dad?_____

How is my relationship to parents and siblings?_____

_____

_____

MENTOR MEETING

Parent and Child Relationship

Date: _____ Parent Conducting: _____

Exciting News: _____

Calendar

Monday	Tuesday	Wednesday	Thursday	Friday	Saturday	Sunday

Progress on Spiritual Goals: _____

New Spiritual Goal: _____

Progress on previous Educational Goals/commitments: _____

New Educational Goals: _____

_____

Personal Growth (Behaviors / Concerns / Decisions / Skills): _____

_____

Social Goals (Family / Friends / Boundaries) _____

_____

This week's Educational Goals: _____

_____

New commitments: I, _____ commit to _____

Signed: _____ Witnessed: _____

Fun Goal for the week: _____

Date with Dad/Mom, if it applies: _____

What do I need from Mom/Dad? _____

How is my relationship to parents and siblings? _____

_____

_____

MENTOR MEETING
Parent and Child Relationship

Date: _____ Parent Conducting: _____

Exciting News: _____

Calendar

Monday	Tuesday	Wednesday	Thursday	Friday	Saturday	Sunday

Progress on Spiritual Goals: _____

New Spiritual Goal: _____

Progress on previous Educational Goals/commitments: _____

New Educational Goals: _____

_____

Personal Growth (Behaviors / Concerns / Decisions / Skills): _____

_____

Social Goals (Family / Friends / Boundaries) _____

_____

This week's Educational Goals: _____

_____

New commitments: I, _____ commit to _____

Signed: _____ Witnessed: _____

Fun Goal for the week: _____

Date with Dad/Mom, if it applies: _____

What do I need from Mom/Dad? _____

How is my relationship to parents and siblings? _____

_____

_____

MENTOR MEETING
Parent and Child Relationship

Date: _____ Parent Conducting: _____

Exciting News: _____
Calendar

Monday	Tuesday	Wednesday	Thursday	Friday	Saturday	Sunday

Progress on Spiritual Goals: _____

New Spiritual Goal: _____

Progress on previous Educational Goals/commitments: _____

New Educational Goals: _____

_____

Personal Growth (Behaviors / Concerns / Decisions / Skills): _____

_____

Social Goals (Family / Friends / Boundaries) _____

_____

This week's Educational Goals: _____

_____

New commitments: I, _____ commit to _____

Signed: _____ Witnessed: _____

Fun Goal for the week: _____

Date with Dad/Mom, if it applies: _____

What do I need from Mom/Dad? _____

How is my relationship to parents and siblings? _____

_____

_____

MENTOR MEETING
Parent and Child Relationship

Date: _____ Parent Conducting: _____

Exciting News: _____

Calendar

Monday	Tuesday	Wednesday	Thursday	Friday	Saturday	Sunday

Progress on Spiritual Goals: _____

New Spiritual Goal: _____

Progress on previous Educational Goals/commitments: _____

New Educational Goals: _____

_____

Personal Growth (Behaviors / Concerns / Decisions / Skills): _____

_____

Social Goals (Family / Friends / Boundaries) _____

_____

This week's Educational Goals: _____

_____

New commitments: I, _____ commit to _____

Signed: _____ Witnessed: _____

Fun Goal for the week: _____

Date with Dad/Mom, if it applies: _____

What do I need from Mom/Dad? _____

How is my relationship to parents and siblings? _____

_____

_____

MENTOR MEETING
Parent and Child Relationship

Date: _____ Parent Conducting: _____

Exciting News: _____

Calendar

Monday	Tuesday	Wednesday	Thursday	Friday	Saturday	Sunday

Progress on Spiritual Goals: _____

New Spiritual Goal: _____

Progress on previous Educational Goals/commitments: _____

New Educational Goals: _____
_____

Personal Growth (Behaviors / Concerns / Decisions / Skills): _____
_____

Social Goals (Family / Friends / Boundaries) _____
_____

This week's Educational Goals: _____
_____

New commitments: I, _____ commit to _____

Signed: _____ Witnessed: _____

Fun Goal for the week: _____

Date with Dad/Mom, if it applies: _____

What do I need from Mom/Dad? _____

How is my relationship to parents and siblings? _____
_____
_____

MENTOR MEETING

Parent and Child Relationship

Date:_____ Parent Conducting:_____

Exciting News:_____

Calendar

Monday	Tuesday	Wednesday	Thursday	Friday	Saturday	Sunday

Progress on Spiritual Goals:_____

New Spiritual Goal:_____

Progress on previous Educational Goals/commitments:_____

New Educational Goals:_____

_____

Personal Growth (Behaviors / Concerns / Decisions / Skills):_____

_____

Social Goals (Family / Friends / Boundaries)_____

_____

This week's Educational Goals:_____

_____

New commitments: I,_____ commit to _____

Signed:_____ Witnessed:_____

Fun Goal for the week:_____

Date with Dad/Mom, if it applies:_____

What do I need from Mom/Dad?_____

How is my relationship to parents and siblings?_____

_____

_____

MENTOR MEETING

Parent and Child Relationship

Date: _____   Parent Conducting: _____

Exciting News: _____
Calendar

Monday	Tuesday	Wednesday	Thursday	Friday	Saturday	Sunday

Progress on Spiritual Goals: _____

New Spiritual Goal: _____

Progress on previous Educational Goals/commitments: _____

New Educational Goals: _____

_____

Personal Growth (Behaviors / Concerns / Decisions / Skills): _____

_____

Social Goals (Family / Friends / Boundaries) _____

_____

This week's Educational Goals: _____

_____

New commitments: I, _____ commit to _____

Signed: _____   Witnessed: _____

Fun Goal for the week: _____

Date with Dad/Mom, if it applies: _____

What do I need from Mom/Dad? _____

How is my relationship to parents and siblings? _____

_____

_____

MENTOR MEETING
Parent and Child Relationship

Date:_____ Parent Conducting:_____

Exciting News:_____

Calendar

Monday	Tuesday	Wednesday	Thursday	Friday	Saturday	Sunday

Progress on Spiritual Goals:_____

New Spiritual Goal:_____

Progress on previous Educational Goals/commitments:_____

New Educational Goals:_____

_____

Personal Growth (Behaviors / Concerns / Decisions / Skills):_____

_____

Social Goals (Family / Friends / Boundaries)_____

_____

This week's Educational Goals:_____

_____

New commitments: I,_____ commit to _____

Signed:_____ Witnessed:_____

Fun Goal for the week:_____

Date with Dad/Mom, if it applies:_____

What do I need from Mom/Dad?_____

How is my relationship to parents and siblings?_____

_____

_____

MENTOR MEETING
Parent and Child Relationship

Date: _____ Parent Conducting: _____

Exciting News: _____

Calendar

Monday	Tuesday	Wednesday	Thursday	Friday	Saturday	Sunday

Progress on Spiritual Goals: _____

New Spiritual Goal: _____

Progress on previous Educational Goals/commitments: _____

New Educational Goals: _____

Personal Growth (Behaviors / Concerns / Decisions / Skills): _____

Social Goals (Family / Friends / Boundaries) _____

This week's Educational Goals: _____

New commitments: I, _____ commit to _____

Signed: _____ Witnessed: _____

Fun Goal for the week: _____

Date with Dad/Mom, if it applies: _____

What do I need from Mom/Dad? _____

How is my relationship to parents and siblings? _____

MENTOR MEETING
Parent and Child Relationship

Date:_____ Parent Conducting: _____

Exciting News: _____

Calendar

Monday	Tuesday	Wednesday	Thursday	Friday	Saturday	Sunday

Progress on Spiritual Goals:_____

New Spiritual Goal: _____

Progress on previous Educational Goals/commitments: _____

New Educational Goals: _____

Personal Growth (Behaviors / Concerns / Decisions / Skills): _____

Social Goals (Family / Friends / Boundaries)_____

This week's Educational Goals:_____

New commitments: I,_____ commit to _____

Signed:_____ Witnessed: _____

Fun Goal for the week: _____

Date with Dad/Mom, if it applies: _____

What do I need from Mom/Dad? _____

How is my relationship to parents and siblings?_____

_____

MENTOR MEETING
Parent and Child Relationship

Date: _____   Parent Conducting: _____

Exciting News: _____

Calendar

Monday	Tuesday	Wednesday	Thursday	Friday	Saturday	Sunday

Progress on Spiritual Goals: _____

New Spiritual Goal: _____

Progress on previous Educational Goals/commitments: _____

New Educational Goals: _____

_____

Personal Growth (Behaviors / Concerns / Decisions / Skills): _____

_____

Social Goals (Family / Friends / Boundaries) _____

_____

This week's Educational Goals: _____

_____

New commitments: I, _____ commit to _____

Signed: _____   Witnessed: _____

Fun Goal for the week: _____

Date with Dad/Mom, if it applies: _____

What do I need from Mom/Dad? _____

How is my relationship to parents and siblings? _____

_____

_____

MENTOR MEETING
Parent and Child Relationship

Date:_____   Parent Conducting:_____

Exciting News:_____

Calendar

Monday	Tuesday	Wednesday	Thursday	Friday	Saturday	Sunday

Progress on Spiritual Goals:_____

New Spiritual Goal:_____

Progress on previous Educational Goals/commitments:_____

New Educational Goals:_____

_____

Personal Growth (Behaviors / Concerns / Decisions / Skills):_____

_____

Social Goals (Family / Friends / Boundaries)_____

_____

This week's Educational Goals:_____

_____

New commitments: I,_____ commit to _____

Signed:_____   Witnessed:_____

Fun Goal for the week:_____

Date with Dad/Mom, if it applies:_____

What do I need from Mom/Dad?_____

How is my relationship to parents and siblings?_____

_____

_____

MENTOR MEETING
Parent and Child Relationship

Date: _____   Parent Conducting: _____

Exciting News: _____

Calendar

Monday	Tuesday	Wednesday	Thursday	Friday	Saturday	Sunday

Progress on Spiritual Goals: _____

New Spiritual Goal: _____

Progress on previous Educational Goals/commitments: _____

New Educational Goals: _____

_____

Personal Growth (Behaviors / Concerns / Decisions / Skills): _____

_____

Social Goals (Family / Friends / Boundaries) _____

_____

This week's Educational Goals: _____

_____

New commitments: I, _____ commit to _____

Signed: _____   Witnessed: _____

Fun Goal for the week: _____

Date with Dad/Mom, if it applies: _____

What do I need from Mom/Dad? _____

How is my relationship to parents and siblings? _____

_____

_____

MENTOR MEETING

Parent and Child Relationship

Date:_____ Parent Conducting:_____

Exciting News:_____

Calendar

Monday	Tuesday	Wednesday	Thursday	Friday	Saturday	Sunday

Progress on Spiritual Goals:_____

New Spiritual Goal:_____

Progress on previous Educational Goals/commitments:_____

New Educational Goals:_____

_____

Personal Growth (Behaviors / Concerns / Decisions / Skills):_____

_____

Social Goals (Family / Friends / Boundaries)_____

_____

This week's Educational Goals:_____

_____

New commitments: I,_____ commit to _____

Signed:_____ Witnessed:_____

Fun Goal for the week:_____

Date with Dad/Mom, if it applies:_____

What do I need from Mom/Dad?_____

How is my relationship to parents and siblings?_____

_____

_____

MENTOR MEETING

Parent and Child Relationship

Date: _____   Parent Conducting: _____

Exciting News: _____

Calendar

Monday	Tuesday	Wednesday	Thursday	Friday	Saturday	Sunday

Progress on Spiritual Goals: _____

New Spiritual Goal: _____

Progress on previous Educational Goals/commitments: _____

New Educational Goals: _____

_____

Personal Growth (Behaviors / Concerns / Decisions / Skills): _____

_____

Social Goals (Family / Friends / Boundaries) _____

_____

This week's Educational Goals: _____

_____

New commitments: I, _____ commit to _____

Signed: _____ Witnessed: _____

Fun Goal for the week: _____

Date with Dad/Mom, if it applies: _____

What do I need from Mom/Dad? _____

How is my relationship to parents and siblings? _____

_____

_____

MENTOR MEETING
Parent and Child Relationship

Date: _____ Parent Conducting: _____

Exciting News: _____

Calendar

Monday	Tuesday	Wednesday	Thursday	Friday	Saturday	Sunday

Progress on Spiritual Goals: _____

New Spiritual Goal: _____

Progress on previous Educational Goals/commitments: _____

New Educational Goals: _____

_____

Personal Growth (Behaviors / Concerns / Decisions / Skills): _____

_____

Social Goals (Family / Friends / Boundaries) _____

_____

This week's Educational Goals: _____

_____

New commitments: I, _____ commit to _____

Signed: _____ Witnessed: _____

Fun Goal for the week: _____

Date with Dad/Mom, if it applies: _____

What do I need from Mom/Dad? _____

How is my relationship to parents and siblings? _____

_____

_____

MENTOR MEETING
Parent and Child Relationship

Date: _____   Parent Conducting: _____

Exciting News: _____
Calendar

Monday	Tuesday	Wednesday	Thursday	Friday	Saturday	Sunday

Progress on Spiritual Goals: _____

New Spiritual Goal: _____

Progress on previous Educational Goals/commitments: _____

New Educational Goals: _____

_____

Personal Growth (Behaviors / Concerns / Decisions / Skills): _____

_____

Social Goals (Family / Friends / Boundaries) _____

_____

This week's Educational Goals: _____

_____

New commitments: I, _____ commit to _____

Signed: _____ Witnessed: _____

Fun Goal for the week: _____

Date with Dad/Mom, if it applies: _____

What do I need from Mom/Dad? _____

How is my relationship to parents and siblings? _____

_____

_____

MENTOR MEETING

Parent and Child Relationship

Date: _____ Parent Conducting: _____

Exciting News: _____

Calendar

Monday	Tuesday	Wednesday	Thursday	Friday	Saturday	Sunday

Progress on Spiritual Goals: _____

New Spiritual Goal: _____

Progress on previous Educational Goals/commitments: _____

New Educational Goals: _____

_____

Personal Growth (Behaviors / Concerns / Decisions / Skills): _____

_____

Social Goals (Family / Friends / Boundaries) _____

_____

This week's Educational Goals: _____

_____

New commitments: I, _____ commit to _____

Signed: _____ Witnessed: _____

Fun Goal for the week: _____

Date with Dad/Mom, if it applies: _____

What do I need from Mom/Dad? _____

How is my relationship to parents and siblings? _____

_____

_____

MENTOR MEETING
Parent and Child Relationship

Date: _____   Parent Conducting: _____

Exciting News: _____
          Calendar

Monday	Tuesday	Wednesday	Thursday	Friday	Saturday	Sunday

Progress on Spiritual Goals: _____

New Spiritual Goal: _____

Progress on previous Educational Goals/commitments: _____

New Educational Goals: _____

_____

Personal Growth (Behaviors / Concerns / Decisions / Skills): _____

_____

Social Goals (Family / Friends / Boundaries) _____

_____

This week's Educational Goals: _____

_____

New commitments: I, _____ commit to _____

Signed: _____   Witnessed: _____

Fun Goal for the week: _____

Date with Dad/Mom, if it applies: _____

What do I need from Mom/Dad? _____

How is my relationship to parents and siblings? _____

_____

_____

MENTOR MEETING
Parent and Child Relationship

Date:_____ Parent Conducting:_____

Exciting News:_____
Calendar

Monday	Tuesday	Wednesday	Thursday	Friday	Saturday	Sunday

Progress on Spiritual Goals:_____

New Spiritual Goal:_____

Progress on previous Educational Goals/commitments:_____

New Educational Goals:_____

_____

Personal Growth (Behaviors / Concerns / Decisions / Skills):_____

_____

Social Goals (Family / Friends / Boundaries)_____

_____

This week's Educational Goals:_____

_____

New commitments: I,_____ commit to _____

Signed:_____ Witnessed:_____

Fun Goal for the week:_____

Date with Dad/Mom, if it applies:_____

What do I need from Mom/Dad?_____

How is my relationship to parents and siblings?_____

_____

_____

MENTOR MEETING
Parent and Child Relationship

Date: _____   Parent Conducting: _____

Exciting News: _____

Calendar

Monday	Tuesday	Wednesday	Thursday	Friday	Saturday	Sunday

Progress on Spiritual Goals: _____

New Spiritual Goal: _____

Progress on previous Educational Goals/commitments: _____

New Educational Goals: _____

_____

Personal Growth (Behaviors / Concerns / Decisions / Skills): _____

_____

Social Goals (Family / Friends / Boundaries) _____

_____

This week's Educational Goals: _____

_____

New commitments: I, _____ commit to _____

Signed: _____   Witnessed: _____

Fun Goal for the week: _____

Date with Dad/Mom, if it applies: _____

What do I need from Mom/Dad? _____

How is my relationship to parents and siblings? _____

_____

_____

MENTOR MEETING
Parent and Child Relationship

Date: _____ Parent Conducting: _____

Exciting News: _____

Calendar

Monday	Tuesday	Wednesday	Thursday	Friday	Saturday	Sunday

Progress on Spiritual Goals: _____

New Spiritual Goal: _____

Progress on previous Educational Goals/commitments: _____

New Educational Goals: _____

_____

Personal Growth (Behaviors / Concerns / Decisions / Skills): _____

_____

Social Goals (Family / Friends / Boundaries) _____

_____

This week's Educational Goals: _____

_____

New commitments: I, _____ commit to _____

Signed: _____ Witnessed: _____

Fun Goal for the week: _____

Date with Dad/Mom, if it applies: _____

What do I need from Mom/Dad? _____

How is my relationship to parents and siblings? _____

_____

_____

MENTOR MEETING
Parent and Child Relationship

Date: _____   Parent Conducting: _____

Exciting News: _____
Calendar

Monday	Tuesday	Wednesday	Thursday	Friday	Saturday	Sunday

Progress on Spiritual Goals: _____

New Spiritual Goal: _____

Progress on previous Educational Goals/commitments: _____

New Educational Goals: _____

_____

Personal Growth (Behaviors / Concerns / Decisions / Skills): _____

_____

Social Goals (Family / Friends / Boundaries) _____

_____

This week's Educational Goals: _____

_____

New commitments: I, _____ commit to _____

Signed: _____ Witnessed: _____

Fun Goal for the week: _____

Date with Dad/Mom, if it applies: _____

What do I need from Mom/Dad? _____

How is my relationship to parents and siblings? _____

_____

_____

MENTOR MEETING
Parent and Child Relationship

Date:_____ Parent Conducting:_____

Exciting News:_____
Calendar

Monday	Tuesday	Wednesday	Thursday	Friday	Saturday	Sunday

Progress on Spiritual Goals:_____

New Spiritual Goal:_____

Progress on previous Educational Goals/commitments:_____

New Educational Goals:_____

_____

Personal Growth (Behaviors / Concerns / Decisions / Skills):_____

_____

Social Goals (Family / Friends / Boundaries)_____

_____

This week's Educational Goals:_____

_____

New commitments: I,_____ commit to _____

Signed:_____ Witnessed:_____

Fun Goal for the week:_____

Date with Dad/Mom, if it applies:_____

What do I need from Mom/Dad?_____

How is my relationship to parents and siblings?_____

_____

_____

MENTOR MEETING

Parent and Child Relationship

Date: _____ Parent Conducting: _____

Exciting News: _____
Calendar

Monday	Tuesday	Wednesday	Thursday	Friday	Saturday	Sunday

Progress on Spiritual Goals: _____

New Spiritual Goal: _____

Progress on previous Educational Goals/commitments: _____

New Educational Goals: _____

_____

Personal Growth (Behaviors / Concerns / Decisions / Skills): _____

_____

Social Goals (Family / Friends / Boundaries) _____

_____

This week's Educational Goals: _____

_____

New commitments: I, _____ commit to _____

Signed: _____ Witnessed: _____

Fun Goal for the week: _____

Date with Dad/Mom, if it applies: _____

What do I need from Mom/Dad? _____

How is my relationship to parents and siblings? _____

_____

_____

MENTOR MEETING
Parent and Child Relationship

Date:_____ Parent Conducting:_____

Exciting News:_____

Calendar

Monday	Tuesday	Wednesday	Thursday	Friday	Saturday	Sunday

Progress on Spiritual Goals:_____

New Spiritual Goal: _____

Progress on previous Educational Goals/commitments: _____

New Educational Goals:_____

_____

Personal Growth (Behaviors / Concerns / Decisions / Skills):_____

_____

Social Goals (Family / Friends / Boundaries)_____

_____

This week's Educational Goals:_____

_____

New commitments: I,_____ commit to _____

Signed:_____ Witnessed:_____

Fun Goal for the week:_____

Date with Dad/Mom, if it applies: _____

What do I need from Mom/Dad?_____

How is my relationship to parents and siblings?_____

_____

_____

MENTOR MEETING

Parent and Child Relationship

Date: _____   Parent Conducting: _____

Exciting News: _____

Calendar

Monday	Tuesday	Wednesday	Thursday	Friday	Saturday	Sunday

Progress on Spiritual Goals: _____

New Spiritual Goal: _____

Progress on previous Educational Goals/commitments: _____

New Educational Goals: _____
_____

Personal Growth (Behaviors / Concerns / Decisions / Skills): _____
_____

Social Goals (Family / Friends / Boundaries) _____
_____

This week's Educational Goals: _____
_____

New commitments: I, _____ commit to _____

Signed: _____   Witnessed: _____

Fun Goal for the week: _____

Date with Dad/Mom, if it applies: _____

What do I need from Mom/Dad? _____

How is my relationship to parents and siblings? _____
_____
_____

MENTOR MEETING
Parent and Child Relationship

Date:_____ Parent Conducting: _____

Exciting News: _____
Calendar

Monday	Tuesday	Wednesday	Thursday	Friday	Saturday	Sunday

Progress on Spiritual Goals:_____

New Spiritual Goal: _____

Progress on previous Educational Goals/commitments:_____

New Educational Goals: _____

_____

Personal Growth (Behaviors / Concerns / Decisions / Skills):_____

_____

Social Goals (Family / Friends / Boundaries)_____

_____

This week's Educational Goals:_____

_____

New commitments: I,_____ commit to _____

Signed:_____ Witnessed: _____

Fun Goal for the week:_____

Date with Dad/Mom, if it applies: _____

What do I need from Mom/Dad?_____

How is my relationship to parents and siblings?_____

_____

_____

MENTOR MEETING
Parent and Child Relationship

Date: _____   Parent Conducting: _____

Exciting News: _____

Calendar

Monday	Tuesday	Wednesday	Thursday	Friday	Saturday	Sunday

Progress on Spiritual Goals: _____

New Spiritual Goal: _____

Progress on previous Educational Goals/commitments: _____

New Educational Goals: _____

_____

Personal Growth (Behaviors / Concerns / Decisions / Skills): _____

_____

Social Goals (Family / Friends / Boundaries) _____

_____

This week's Educational Goals: _____

_____

New commitments: I, _____ commit to _____

Signed: _____   Witnessed: _____

Fun Goal for the week: _____

Date with Dad/Mom, if it applies: _____

What do I need from Mom/Dad? _____

How is my relationship to parents and siblings? _____

_____

_____

MENTOR MEETING
Parent and Child Relationship

Date:_____ Parent Conducting:_____

Exciting News:_____
Calendar

Monday	Tuesday	Wednesday	Thursday	Friday	Saturday	Sunday

Progress on Spiritual Goals:_____

New Spiritual Goal:_____

Progress on previous Educational Goals/commitments:_____

New Educational Goals:_____
_____

Personal Growth (Behaviors / Concerns / Decisions / Skills):_____
_____

Social Goals (Family / Friends / Boundaries)_____
_____

This week's Educational Goals:_____
_____

New commitments: I,_____ commit to _____

Signed:_____ Witnessed:_____

Fun Goal for the week:_____

Date with Dad/Mom, if it applies: _____

What do I need from Mom/Dad?_____

How is my relationship to parents and siblings?_____
_____
_____

MENTOR MEETING

Parent and Child Relationship

Date: _____   Parent Conducting: _____

Exciting News: _____

Calendar

Monday	Tuesday	Wednesday	Thursday	Friday	Saturday	Sunday

Progress on Spiritual Goals: _____

New Spiritual Goal: _____

Progress on previous Educational Goals/commitments: _____

New Educational Goals: _____

_____

Personal Growth (Behaviors / Concerns / Decisions / Skills): _____

_____

Social Goals (Family / Friends / Boundaries) _____

_____

This week's Educational Goals: _____

_____

New commitments: I, _____ commit to _____

Signed: _____ Witnessed: _____

Fun Goal for the week: _____

Date with Dad/Mom, if it applies: _____

What do I need from Mom/Dad? _____

How is my relationship to parents and siblings? _____

_____

_____

MENTOR MEETING

Parent and Child Relationship

Date: _____ Parent Conducting: _____

Exciting News: _____

Calendar

Monday	Tuesday	Wednesday	Thursday	Friday	Saturday	Sunday

Progress on Spiritual Goals: _____

New Spiritual Goal: _____

Progress on previous Educational Goals/commitments: _____

New Educational Goals: _____

_____

Personal Growth (Behaviors / Concerns / Decisions / Skills): _____

_____

Social Goals (Family / Friends / Boundaries) _____

_____

This week's Educational Goals: _____

_____

New commitments: I, _____ commit to _____

Signed: _____ Witnessed: _____

Fun Goal for the week: _____

Date with Dad/Mom, if it applies: _____

What do I need from Mom/Dad? _____

How is my relationship to parents and siblings? _____

_____

_____

MENTOR MEETING
Parent and Child Relationship

Date: _____ Parent Conducting: _____

Exciting News: _____

Calendar

Monday	Tuesday	Wednesday	Thursday	Friday	Saturday	Sunday

Progress on Spiritual Goals:_____

New Spiritual Goal: _____

Progress on previous Educational Goals/commitments: _____

New Educational Goals: _____

_____

Personal Growth (Behaviors / Concerns / Decisions / Skills):_____

_____

Social Goals (Family / Friends / Boundaries)_____

_____

This week's Educational Goals: _____

_____

New commitments: I,_____ commit to _____

Signed: _____ Witnessed: _____

Fun Goal for the week: _____

Date with Dad/Mom, if it applies: _____

What do I need from Mom/Dad? _____

How is my relationship to parents and siblings? _____

_____

_____

MENTOR MEETING
Parent and Child Relationship

Date:_____ Parent Conducting:_____

Exciting News:_____

Calendar

Monday	Tuesday	Wednesday	Thursday	Friday	Saturday	Sunday

Progress on Spiritual Goals:_____

New Spiritual Goal:_____

Progress on previous Educational Goals/commitments:_____

New Educational Goals:_____

_____

Personal Growth (Behaviors / Concerns / Decisions / Skills):_____

_____

Social Goals (Family / Friends / Boundaries)_____

_____

This week's Educational Goals:_____

_____

New commitments: I,_____ commit to _____

Signed:_____ Witnessed:_____

Fun Goal for the week:_____

Date with Dad/Mom, if it applies:_____

What do I need from Mom/Dad?_____

How is my relationship to parents and siblings?_____

_____

_____

MENTOR MEETING
Parent and Child Relationship

Date: _____ Parent Conducting: _____

Exciting News: _____
Calendar

Monday	Tuesday	Wednesday	Thursday	Friday	Saturday	Sunday

Progress on Spiritual Goals: _____

New Spiritual Goal: _____

Progress on previous Educational Goals/commitments: _____

New Educational Goals: _____

_____

Personal Growth (Behaviors / Concerns / Decisions / Skills): _____

_____

Social Goals (Family / Friends / Boundaries) _____

_____

This week's Educational Goals: _____

_____

New commitments: I, _____ commit to _____

Signed: _____ Witnessed: _____

Fun Goal for the week: _____

Date with Dad/Mom, if it applies: _____

What do I need from Mom/Dad? _____

How is my relationship to parents and siblings? _____

_____

_____

MENTOR MEETING
Parent and Child Relationship

Date:_____ Parent Conducting:_____

Exciting News:_____

Calendar

Monday	Tuesday	Wednesday	Thursday	Friday	Saturday	Sunday

Progress on Spiritual Goals:_____

New Spiritual Goal:_____

Progress on previous Educational Goals/commitments:_____

New Educational Goals:_____

_____

Personal Growth (Behaviors / Concerns / Decisions / Skills):_____

_____

Social Goals (Family / Friends / Boundaries)_____

_____

This week's Educational Goals:_____

_____

New commitments: I,_____ commit to _____

Signed:_____ Witnessed:_____

Fun Goal for the week:_____

Date with Dad/Mom, if it applies:_____

What do I need from Mom/Dad?_____

How is my relationship to parents and siblings?_____

_____

_____

MENTOR MEETING
Parent and Child Relationship

Date: _____   Parent Conducting: _____

Exciting News: _____

Calendar

Monday	Tuesday	Wednesday	Thursday	Friday	Saturday	Sunday

Progress on Spiritual Goals: _____

New Spiritual Goal: _____

Progress on previous Educational Goals/commitments: _____

New Educational Goals: _____

_____

Personal Growth (Behaviors / Concerns / Decisions / Skills): _____

_____

Social Goals (Family / Friends / Boundaries) _____

_____

This week's Educational Goals: _____

_____

New commitments: I, _____ commit to _____

Signed: _____   Witnessed: _____

Fun Goal for the week: _____

Date with Dad/Mom, if it applies: _____

What do I need from Mom/Dad? _____

How is my relationship to parents and siblings? _____

_____

_____

MENTOR MEETING
Parent and Child Relationship

Date: _____ Parent Conducting: _____

Exciting News: _____

Calendar

Monday	Tuesday	Wednesday	Thursday	Friday	Saturday	Sunday

Progress on Spiritual Goals:_____

New Spiritual Goal: _____

Progress on previous Educational Goals/commitments: _____

New Educational Goals: _____
_____

Personal Growth (Behaviors / Concerns / Decisions / Skills):_____
_____

Social Goals (Family / Friends / Boundaries)_____
_____

This week's Educational Goals:_____
_____

New commitments: I,_____ commit to _____

Signed:_____ Witnessed:_____

Fun Goal for the week: _____

Date with Dad/Mom, if it applies: _____

What do I need from Mom/Dad?_____

How is my relationship to parents and siblings?_____
_____
_____

MENTOR MEETING
Parent and Child Relationship

Date: _____   Parent Conducting: _____

Exciting News: _____

Calendar

Monday	Tuesday	Wednesday	Thursday	Friday	Saturday	Sunday

Progress on Spiritual Goals: _____

New Spiritual Goal: _____

Progress on previous Educational Goals/commitments: _____

New Educational Goals: _____

_____

Personal Growth (Behaviors / Concerns / Decisions / Skills): _____

_____

Social Goals (Family / Friends / Boundaries) _____

_____

This week's Educational Goals: _____

_____

New commitments: I, _____ commit to _____

Signed: _____   Witnessed: _____

Fun Goal for the week: _____

Date with Dad/Mom, if it applies: _____

What do I need from Mom/Dad? _____

How is my relationship to parents and siblings? _____

_____

_____

MENTOR MEETING
Parent and Child Relationship

Date:_____ Parent Conducting:_____

Exciting News:_____
Calendar

Monday	Tuesday	Wednesday	Thursday	Friday	Saturday	Sunday

Progress on Spiritual Goals:_____

New Spiritual Goal:_____

Progress on previous Educational Goals/commitments:_____

New Educational Goals:_____

_____

Personal Growth (Behaviors / Concerns / Decisions / Skills):_____

_____

Social Goals (Family / Friends / Boundaries)_____

_____

This week's Educational Goals:_____

_____

New commitments: I,_____ commit to _____

Signed:_____ Witnessed:_____

Fun Goal for the week:_____

Date with Dad/Mom, if it applies:_____

What do I need from Mom/Dad?_____

How is my relationship to parents and siblings?_____

_____

_____

MENTOR MEETING

Parent and Child Relationship

Date: _____ Parent Conducting: _____

Exciting News: _____

Calendar

Monday	Tuesday	Wednesday	Thursday	Friday	Saturday	Sunday

Progress on Spiritual Goals: _____

New Spiritual Goal: _____

Progress on previous Educational Goals/commitments: _____

New Educational Goals: _____

_____

Personal Growth (Behaviors / Concerns / Decisions / Skills): _____

_____

Social Goals (Family / Friends / Boundaries) _____

_____

This week's Educational Goals: _____

_____

New commitments: I, _____ commit to _____

Signed: _____ Witnessed: _____

Fun Goal for the week: _____

Date with Dad/Mom, if it applies: _____

What do I need from Mom/Dad? _____

How is my relationship to parents and siblings? _____

_____

_____

MENTOR MEETING
Parent and Child Relationship

Date:_____ Parent Conducting:_____

Exciting News:_____
        Calendar

Monday	Tuesday	Wednesday	Thursday	Friday	Saturday	Sunday

Progress on Spiritual Goals:_____

New Spiritual Goal:_____

Progress on previous Educational Goals/commitments:_____

New Educational Goals:_____

_____

Personal Growth (Behaviors / Concerns / Decisions / Skills):_____

_____

Social Goals (Family / Friends / Boundaries)_____

_____

This week's Educational Goals:_____

_____

New commitments: I,_____ commit to _____

Signed:_____ Witnessed:_____

Fun Goal for the week:_____

Date with Dad/Mom, if it applies:_____

What do I need from Mom/Dad?_____

How is my relationship to parents and siblings?_____

_____

_____

MENTOR MEETING

Parent and Child Relationship

Date: _____   Parent Conducting: _____

Exciting News: _____

Calendar

Monday	Tuesday	Wednesday	Thursday	Friday	Saturday	Sunday

Progress on Spiritual Goals:_____

New Spiritual Goal:_____

Progress on previous Educational Goals/commitments: _____

New Educational Goals: _____

_____

Personal Growth (Behaviors / Concerns / Decisions / Skills):_____

_____

Social Goals (Family / Friends / Boundaries)_____

_____

This week's Educational Goals:_____

_____

New commitments: I,_____ commit to _____

Signed: _____   Witnessed: _____

Fun Goal for the week: _____

Date with Dad/Mom, if it applies: _____

What do I need from Mom/Dad? _____

How is my relationship to parents and siblings? _____

_____

_____

MENTOR MEETING
Parent and Child Relationship

Date:_____ Parent Conducting:_____

Exciting News:_____
Calendar

Monday	Tuesday	Wednesday	Thursday	Friday	Saturday	Sunday

Progress on Spiritual Goals:_____

New Spiritual Goal:_____

Progress on previous Educational Goals/commitments:_____

New Educational Goals:_____

_____

Personal Growth (Behaviors / Concerns / Decisions / Skills):_____

_____

Social Goals (Family / Friends / Boundaries)_____

_____

This week's Educational Goals:_____

_____

New commitments: I,_____ commit to _____

Signed:_____ Witnessed:_____

Fun Goal for the week:_____

Date with Dad/Mom, if it applies:_____

What do I need from Mom/Dad?_____

How is my relationship to parents and siblings?_____

_____

_____

MENTOR MEETING
Parent and Child Relationship

Date: _____ Parent Conducting: _____

Exciting News: _____

Calendar

Monday	Tuesday	Wednesday	Thursday	Friday	Saturday	Sunday

Progress on Spiritual Goals:_____

New Spiritual Goal: _____

Progress on previous Educational Goals/commitments: _____

New Educational Goals: _____

_____

Personal Growth (Behaviors / Concerns / Decisions / Skills):_____

_____

Social Goals (Family / Friends / Boundaries)_____

_____

This week's Educational Goals:_____

_____

New commitments: I,_____ commit to _____

Signed: _____ Witnessed: _____

Fun Goal for the week: _____

Date with Dad/Mom, if it applies: _____

What do I need from Mom/Dad? _____

How is my relationship to parents and siblings? _____

_____

_____

MENTOR MEETING
Parent and Child Relationship

Date:_____ Parent Conducting:_____

Exciting News:_____

Calendar

Monday	Tuesday	Wednesday	Thursday	Friday	Saturday	Sunday

Progress on Spiritual Goals:_____

New Spiritual Goal:_____

Progress on previous Educational Goals/commitments:_____

New Educational Goals:_____

_____

Personal Growth (Behaviors / Concerns / Decisions / Skills):_____

_____

Social Goals (Family / Friends / Boundaries)_____

_____

This week's Educational Goals:_____

_____

New commitments: I,_____ commit to _____

Signed:_____ Witnessed:_____

Fun Goal for the week:_____

Date with Dad/Mom, if it applies:_____

What do I need from Mom/Dad?_____

How is my relationship to parents and siblings?_____

_____

_____

MENTOR MEETING

Parent and Child Relationship

Date: _____ Parent Conducting: _____

Exciting News: _____

Calendar

Monday	Tuesday	Wednesday	Thursday	Friday	Saturday	Sunday

Progress on Spiritual Goals: _____

New Spiritual Goal: _____

Progress on previous Educational Goals/commitments: _____

New Educational Goals: _____

_____

Personal Growth (Behaviors / Concerns / Decisions / Skills): _____

_____

Social Goals (Family / Friends / Boundaries) _____

_____

This week's Educational Goals: _____

_____

New commitments: I, _____ commit to _____

Signed: _____ Witnessed: _____

Fun Goal for the week: _____

Date with Dad/Mom, if it applies: _____

What do I need from Mom/Dad? _____

How is my relationship to parents and siblings? _____

_____

_____

MENTOR MEETING
Parent and Child Relationship

Date:_____ Parent Conducting:_____

Exciting News:_____

Calendar

Monday	Tuesday	Wednesday	Thursday	Friday	Saturday	Sunday

Progress on Spiritual Goals:_____

New Spiritual Goal:_____

Progress on previous Educational Goals/commitments:_____

New Educational Goals:_____
_____

Personal Growth (Behaviors / Concerns / Decisions / Skills):_____
_____

Social Goals (Family / Friends / Boundaries)_____
_____

This week's Educational Goals:_____
_____

New commitments: I,_____ commit to _____

Signed:_____ Witnessed:_____

Fun Goal for the week:_____

Date with Dad/Mom, if it applies:_____

What do I need from Mom/Dad?_____

How is my relationship to parents and siblings?_____
_____
_____

MENTOR MEETING

Parent and Child Relationship

Date: _____ Parent Conducting: _____

Exciting News: _____

Calendar

Monday	Tuesday	Wednesday	Thursday	Friday	Saturday	Sunday

Progress on Spiritual Goals: _____

New Spiritual Goal: _____

Progress on previous Educational Goals/commitments: _____

New Educational Goals: _____

_____

Personal Growth (Behaviors / Concerns / Decisions / Skills): _____

_____

Social Goals (Family / Friends / Boundaries) _____

_____

This week's Educational Goals: _____

_____

New commitments: I, _____ commit to _____

Signed: _____ Witnessed: _____

Fun Goal for the week: _____

Date with Dad/Mom, if it applies: _____

What do I need from Mom/Dad? _____

How is my relationship to parents and siblings? _____

_____

_____

MENTOR MEETING
Parent and Child Relationship

Date:_____ Parent Conducting:_____

Exciting News:_____

Calendar

Monday	Tuesday	Wednesday	Thursday	Friday	Saturday	Sunday

Progress on Spiritual Goals:_____

New Spiritual Goal:_____

Progress on previous Educational Goals/commitments:_____

New Educational Goals:_____
_____

Personal Growth (Behaviors / Concerns / Decisions / Skills):_____
_____

Social Goals (Family / Friends / Boundaries)_____
_____

This week's Educational Goals:_____
_____

New commitments: I,_____ commit to _____

Signed:_____ Witnessed:_____

Fun Goal for the week:_____

Date with Dad/Mom, if it applies:_____

What do I need from Mom/Dad?_____

How is my relationship to parents and siblings?_____
_____
_____

MENTOR MEETING

Parent and Child Relationship

Date: _____   Parent Conducting: _____

Exciting News: _____

Calendar

Monday	Tuesday	Wednesday	Thursday	Friday	Saturday	Sunday

Progress on Spiritual Goals: _____

New Spiritual Goal: _____

Progress on previous Educational Goals/commitments: _____

New Educational Goals: _____

_____

Personal Growth (Behaviors / Concerns / Decisions / Skills): _____

_____

Social Goals (Family / Friends / Boundaries) _____

_____

This week's Educational Goals: _____

_____

New commitments: I, _____ commit to _____

Signed: _____ Witnessed: _____

Fun Goal for the week: _____

Date with Dad/Mom, if it applies: _____

What do I need from Mom/Dad? _____

How is my relationship to parents and siblings? _____

_____

_____

ABOUT THE AUTHOR

When it comes to parenting, Nicholeen Peck is a worldwide phenomenon and leader — and for good reason! Her proven system based on Four Simple Skills transforms even the most out-of-control teenagers and homes from chaos to calm within days. Though she's an international speaker, author, mentor, former foster parent of many difficult and troubled teens, and even President of the Worldwide Organization for Women (an approved consultant for the United Nations), Nicholeen spends most of her free time at home with her husband having raised her four children — which she knows will be her greatest impact and legacy, and loves spending time with them and her grandchildren. The fact that she has had such an international influence while still being a stay-at-home mom is evidence of the effectiveness of her teachings. Learn more about her mission and methods at www.teachingselfgovernment.com.

RESOURCES TO IMPLEMENT
TEACHING SELF-GOVERNMENT PRINCIPLES
IN YOUR HOME

If you want help implementing the Teaching Self-Government principles into your home, or would like more understanding of how it all works, then...

The Teaching Self-Government TSG PARENTING COURSE™ is just for you!

The TSG Parenting Course includes:
- Advanced-level classes
- Video of actual parenting interactions
- Weekly group mentor calls with Nicholeen
- A special member forum for Q&A
- Ongoing support

Buy the full course at:
teachingselfgovernment.com/store

Also available at teachingingselfgovernment.com:
- Audio classes
- Family Tutorial Videos of the Aponte family learning Teaching Self-Government
- TSG Circle memberships
- TSG Weekly Support Group
- Children's books
- Cue Cards
- Poster of the Choices Map
- Books
- and more...

Printed in Poland
by Amazon Fulfillment
Poland Sp. z o.o., Wrocław

33765180R00094